119983

D1603789

DATE DUE

MAR 1 2 1979			
NOV 2 9 1982			
MAY 9 1983			
NOV 1 8 1985			
DEC 0 9 1991			
NOV 1 6 1992			
GAYLORD 234			PRINTED IN U. S. A.

LIFE Pacific College
Alumni Library
1100 West Covina Blvd.
San Dimas, CA 91773

The Epistle to the

HEBREWS

The Epistle to the

HEBREWS

From Ritual to Reality

by
William MacDonald

LOIZEAUX BROTHERS
Neptune, New Jersey

FIRST EDITION, MARCH 1972
SECOND PRINTING, APRIL 1976

Copyright © 1971 by William MacDonald

ISBN 0-87213-570-5

Library of Congress Catalog Card Number: 74-140899

PRINTED IN THE UNITED STATES OF AMERICA

27.8707
145e

LIFE Pacific College
Alumni Library
L.I.F.E. College Library
1100 Glendale Blvd. 1100 West Covina Blvd
Los Angeles, Calif. 90026 San Dimas, CA 91773

CONTENTS

ABBREVIATIONS   7

INTRODUCTION   9

CHAPTER 1   15

CHAPTER 2   27

CHAPTER 3   41

CHAPTER 4   51

CHAPTER 5   65

CHAPTER 6   75

CHAPTER 7   93

CHAPTER 8   109

CHAPTER 9   121

CHAPTER 10   141

CHAPTER 11   169

CHAPTER 12   201

CHAPTER 13   225

THE MESSAGE OF THE EPISTLE
        FOR TODAY   239

BIBLIOGRAPHY   243

5

19120

L.I.F.E. College Library
1100 Glendale Blvd.
Los Angeles, Calif. 90026

ABBREVIATIONS

AV   Authorized Version

ASV   American Standard Version

Con   Confraternity of Christian Doctrine New Testament

JND   New Translation of the Holy Scriptures by J. N. Darby

KJV   King James Version

Knox   The New Testament of Our Lord and Saviour, Jesus Christ, translated by Ronald A. Knox

RSV   Revised Standard Version of the Bible, copyrighted 1946 and 1952 by the Division of Christian Education of the National Council of Churches of Christ in the U.S.A., from which Scripture references are taken unless otherwise indicated, and are used by permission.

INTRODUCTION

In a general way, this work deals with the tremendous struggle involved in leaving one religious system for another. There is the violent wrenching of old ties, the stresses and tensions of alienation, and the formidable pressures exerted on the renegade to return.

But in this Epistle the problem was not just a question of leaving an old system for a new one of equal value. Rather it was a matter of leaving Judaism for Christ, and as the writer shows, this involved leaving shadows for the substance, ritual for reality, the prior for the ultimate, the temporary for the permanent — in short, the good for the best.

The problem also involved leaving the popular for the unpopular, the majority for the minority, and the oppressors for the oppressed. And this precipitated many serious problems.

We do not know the identity of the author. Many are convinced it was the Apostle Paul. Others are equally sure it was not. The safest position is to say that we do not know. But this in no way affects the inspiration of the letter; it has always been accepted by Christians as an integral part of God's Word.

We do know that the letter was written sometime between the ascension of Christ in A.D. 33 and the destruction of the Temple in A.D. 70. The Lord Jesus was already seated at the right hand of God in Heaven (Hebrews 10:12); and the argument of the Epistle indicates that the sacrificial system was still being carried on by the Jewish priests in the Temple.

We also know that the letter was written to people of Hebrew background. These Hebrews had heard the gospel preached by the apostles and others during the early days of the Church, and had seen the mighty miracles of the Holy Spirit which confirmed the message. They had responded to the good news in one of three ways:

> Some believed on the Lord Jesus Christ and were genuinely converted.
>
> Some professed to become Christians, were baptized, and took their place in local assemblies. However, they had never been born again by the Spirit of God.
>
> Others flatly rejected the message of salvation.

Our Epistle deals with the first two classes — truly saved Hebrews and those who had nothing but an outward veneer of Christianity.

Now when a Jew left the faith of his forefathers, he was looked on as a turncoat and an apostate, and was often punished with one or more of the following:

> Disinheritance by his family.
>
> Excommunication from the congregation of Israel.
>
> Loss of employment.
>
> Dispossession.
>
> Mental harassment and physical torture.

Public mockery.
Imprisonment.
Martyrdom.

Of course, there was always the escape route. If he would renounce Christ and return to Judaism, he would be spared from further persecution. As we read between the lines of this letter, we can detect some of the strong arguments that were used to persuade him to return to the Jewish fold:

The rich heritage of the prophets.

The prominent ministry of angels in the history of God's ancient people.

Association with the illustrious lawgiver, Moses.

National ties with the brilliant military commander, Joshua.

The glory of the Aaronic priesthood.

The sacred sanctuary where God chose to dwell among His people.

The covenant of the law given by God through Moses.

The divinely appointed furniture in the sanctuary, and the magnificent veil.

The services in the sanctuary, and especially the ritual on the great Day of Atonement. (This was the most important day in the Jewish calendar.)

We can almost hear the first-century Jews presenting all these glories of their ancient, ritualistic religion, then asking with a sneer, "And what do you Christians have?

We have all this. What do you have? Nothing but a simple upper room, a table, and some bread and wine on the table! Do you mean to say that you have left all this — for that?"

The Epistle to the Hebrews is really an answer to the question, *"What do you have?"* In a word the answer is *Christ.* In Him *we have:*

> One who is greater than the prophets.
>
> One who is greater than the angels.
>
> One who is greater than Moses.
>
> One who is greater than Joshua.
>
> One whose priesthood is superior to that of Aaron.
>
> One who serves in a better sanctuary.
>
> One who has introduced a better covenant.
>
> One who is the antitype of the typical furniture and veil.
>
> One whose once-for-all offering of Himself is superior to the repeated sacrifices of bulls and goats.

Just as the stars fade from view in the greater glory of the sun, so the types and shadows of Judaism pale into insignificance before the greater glory of the Person and work of the Lord Jesus.

Yet there was still the problem of persecution. All who professed to be followers of the Lord Jesus faced bitter, fanatical opposition. For true believers this could lead to the peril of discouragement and despair. They therefore needed to be encouraged to have faith in the promises of God. They needed endurance in view of the coming reward.

For those who were only nominal Christians, there was the danger of apostasy. After professing to receive Christ, they might utterly renounce Him and return to ritualistic religion. This was tantamount to trampling on the Son of God, profaning His blood, and insulting the Holy Spirit. For this willful sin there was no repentance or forgiveness. Against this sin there are repeated warnings in the letter to the Hebrews. In 2:1 it is described as drifting away from the message of Christ. In 3:7-19 it is the sin of rebellion or of hardening the heart. In 6:6 it is falling away or committing apostasy. In 10:26 it is the willful or deliberate sin. In 12:16 it is spoken of as selling one's birthright for a single meal. Finally in 12:25 it is called a refusal to hear the One who is speaking from Heaven. But all these warnings are directed against different aspects of the same sin — the sin of apostasy.

As we shall see, the message of the Epistle is as timely today as it was in the first century of the Church. We need to be constantly reminded of the eternal privileges and blessings that are ours in Christ. We need encouragement to endure in spite of opposition and difficulties, and all professing believers need to be warned against reverting to ceremonial religion after having tasted and seen that the Lord is good.

CHAPTER 1

I. *Christ Superior to the Prophets* (1:1-3)
   A. *Prior revelations* (1:1)
      1. *Partial:* In many
      2. *Differential:* and various ways
      3. *Historical:* God spoke of old
      4. *Patriarchal:* to our fathers
      5. *Prophetical:* by the prophets;
   B. *Pre-eminent revelation* (1:2-3)
      1. *Present:* but in these last days He has spoken to us
      2. *Personal:* in [the person of the] Son (JND),
         a. *Appointed Heir:* whom He appointed the heir of all things,
         b. *Universal Creator:* through whom also He created the world.
         c. *Effulgent glory:* who being the effulgence of His glory (ASV),
         d. *Exact image:* and the very image of His substance (ASV),
         e. *Omnipotent Sustainer:* upholding the universe by His word of power.
         f. *Sin-cleansing Sacrifice:* When He had made purification for sins,
         g. *Enthroned Lord:* He sat down at the right hand of the Majesty on high.

1:1. No Epistle of the New Testament comes to the point as quickly as this one. Without benefit of salutation or introduction, the writer plunges into his subject. It seems as if he were constrained by a holy impatience to set forth the superlative glories of the Lord Jesus Christ.

First, he contrasts God's revelation through the prophets with His revelation in His Son. The prophets were divinely inspired spokesmen for God. They were honored servants of Jehovah. The spiritual wealth of their ministry is preserved in the pages of the Old Testament.

Yet their ministry was partial and fragmentary. To each one was committed a certain measure of revelation, but in every case it was incomplete.

Not only was the truth doled out to them in installments; the methods they used in communicating it were diverse. It was presented as law, history, poetry, and prophecy. Sometimes it was oral, sometimes written. Sometimes it was by visions, dreams, symbols, or pantomime. But whatever the method used, the point is that God's former revelations to the Jewish people were preliminary, progressive, and diverse in the manner of presentation.

1:2. The periodic, partial, and differential prophecies of the Old Testament have now been overshadowed by God's pre-eminent and final revelation in the Person of the Son. The prophets were only channels through whom the divine Word was communicated. The Lord Jesus Christ is Himself the final revelation of God to men. As John said, "No one has ever seen God; the only Son, who is in the bosom of the Father, He has made Him known" (John 1:18). The Lord Jesus said concerning Himself, "He who has seen Me has seen the Father" (John 14:9). Christ speaks not only *for* God but *as* God.

To emphasize the infinite superiority of God's Son to the prophets, the writer first presents Him as Heir of all things. This means that the universe belongs to Him by divine appointment and He will soon reign over it.

It was through Him that God created the world. Jesus Christ was the active agent in creation. He brought into being the stellar heavens, the atmospheric heavens, the earth, the human race, and the divine plan of the ages. Every created thing, both spiritual and physical, was made by Him.

1:3. He is the outshining of God's glory, that is, all the perfections that are found in God the Father are found in Him also. It is not just that He reflects the glory of God (RSV) but that He *is*, the effulgence or radiance of His glory (ASV). All the moral and spiritual glories of God are seen in Him.

Further, the Lord Jesus is the exact image of God's essential being. This cannot, of course, refer to physical likeness because God is, in essence, a Spirit. It means that in every conceivable way Christ exactly represents the Father. No closer resemblance could be possible. The Son, being God, reveals to man by His words and ways exactly what God is like.

And He upholds the universe by His word of power. Originally He spoke to bring the worlds into being

(Hebrews 11:3). Still He speaks and His powerful word sustains life, holds matter together, and maintains the universe in proper order. It is by Him that all things hold together (Colossians 1:17). Here is a simple explanation of a profound scientific problem. Scientists grapple to discover what holds molecules together. We learn here that Jesus Christ is the great Sustainer, and He does it by the word of His power.

But the next glory of our Saviour is the most amazing of all — "When He had made purification for sins." The Creator and the Sustainer became the Sin-bearer. In order to create the universe, He only had to speak. In order to maintain and guide the universe, He only has to speak because no moral problem is involved. But in order to put away our sin once for all, He had to die on the cross of Calvary. It is staggering to think that the sovereign Lord would stoop to become the sacrificial Lamb. "Love so amazing, so divine, demands my soul, my life, my all" (Isaac Watts).

Finally we have His exaltation as the enthroned Lord: "He sat down at the right hand of the Majesty on high." He sat down — the posture of rest. This is not the rest following toil, but the rest of satisfaction in a finished work. This posture indicates that the work of redemption has been completed.

The right hand of the Majesty on high is the position of honor. Because of His glorious triumph, God has highly exalted Him. It is also the position of power; in the Scriptures the right hand is associated with strength. The nail-scarred hand of the Saviour holds the scepter of universal dominion.

In following the pathway of our Lord from creation to Calvary and then to glory, it seems that we have quite lost sight of the prophets. Illustrious though they were, they have receded into the shadows. They bore witness to the coming Messiah (Acts 10:43). Now that He has come, they gladly retire from view.

II. *Christ Superior to the Angels* (1:4–2:18)
  A. *His superiority as the Son of God* (1:4-14)
    1. *A higher place than angels:* having become as much superior to angels
    2. *A greater name than angels:* as the name He has obtained is more excellent than theirs.
      a. *Addressed by God as Son:* For to what angel did God ever say, "Thou art My Son, today I have begotten thee"?
      b. *Acknowledged by God as Son:* Or again, "I will be to him a father, and he shall be to Me a son"?
    3. *The object of angelic worship*
      a. *The determined time:* And when He again bringeth . . . the firstborn into the world (ASV)
      b. *The honored Son:* He says, "Let all God's angels worship Him."
      c. *The subservient angels:* Of the angels He says, "Who makes His angels winds, and His servants flames of fire."
    4. *The Son addressed as:* But of the Son He says,
      a. *God:* Thy throne, O God
      b. *Eternal Sovereign:* is for ever and ever,

  c. *Righteous King:* the righteous scepter is the
     scepter of Thy kingdom.
        (1) *Personal uprightness:* Thou hast loved
            righteousness and hated lawlessness;
        (2) *Peerless position:* therefore God, Thy
            God, has anointed Thee with the oil of
            gladness beyond Thy comrades."
  d. *World Creator:*   And, "Thou, Lord, didst
     found the earth in the beginning, and the
     heavens are the work of Thy hands;
        (1) *Creation's perishability:* they will perish,
        (2) *Creator's permanence:* but Thou re-
            mainest;
        (3) *Creation's prospect*
            (a) *To wear out:* they will all grow old
                like a garment;
            (b) *To be folded up:* like a mantle Thou
                wilt roll them up,
            (c) *To be exchanged:* and they will be
                changed.
        (4) *Creator's perpetuity*
            (a) *Changeless:* But Thou art the same,
            (b) *Endless:* and Thy years will never
                end."
5. *The Son promised absolute dominion:* But to
   what angel has He ever said,
   a. *The Son's position:* Sit at My right hand, till
      I make thy enemies a stool for thy feet"?
   b. *The angels' mission:* Are they not all min-

istering spirits sent forth to serve, for the sake
of those who are to obtain salvation?

1:4. The next step in the argument of the Epistle
demonstrates that Christ is superior to the angels. This
was necessary because the Jewish people had a very high
regard for the ministry of angels. After all, the law had
been given through angels (Acts 7:53; Galatians 3:19),
and angelic beings had appeared frequently throughout
the history of God's ancient people. Perhaps it was
argued that in leaving Judaism for Christ, a person
would be cutting himself off from this important fea-
ture of his national and religious heritage. The truth is
that, in gaining Christ, he gained One who is superior to
angels in a twofold sense — first as Son of God (1:4-14)
and then as Son of Man (2:5-18).

Christ has become "as much superior to angels as the
name He has obtained is more excellent than theirs."
This speaks first of an acquired superiority, then of an
inherent superiority.

The acquired superiority results from His resurrection, ascension, and exaltation as Lord and Christ. In
incarnation He was made for a little while lower than
the angels for the suffering of death (2:9). But God has
exalted Him and enthroned Him in highest glory.

His inherent superiority has to do with His eternal
relationship as Son of God. The more excellent name is
the name of Son.

1:5. Two verses are now quoted from the Old Testament identifying the Messiah as God's Son. First, in

Psalm 2:7, God addresses Him as Son: "You are My son; today I have begotten You." In one sense Christ is the eternally begotten Son. In another sense, He was begotten in incarnation. In a third sense, He was begotten in resurrection — the firstborn from the dead (Colossians 1:18). Paul used this verse in the synagogue at Antioch of Pisidia and applied it to Christ's first advent (Acts 13:33).

But the main point is that God never addressed an angel as His Son. Angels collectively are spoken of as sons of God (Job 1:6, Psalm 89:6 ASV Margin), but in that case it means nothing more than creatures. When the Lord Jesus is described as the Son of God, it signifies equality with God.

The second verse is 2 Samuel 7:14 (KJV): "I will be his father, and he shall be My son." Although the words might seem to have reference to Solomon, the Holy Spirit here identifies them as referring to David's greater Son. Here again the argument is that God never spoke of an angel in this way.

1:6. A third way in which Christ is greater than the angels is that He is to be the object of their worship, whereas they are His messengers and servants. To prove his point, the author quotes Deuteronomy 32:43 (Septuagint) and Psalm 97:7 (see JND Margin).

The verse in Deuteronomy looks forward to the time "when He again bringeth the firstborn into the world" (ASV). In other words, it refers to the second advent of Christ. At that time He will be publicly worshiped by the angels. This can only mean that He is God. It is idolatry to worship any but the true God. Yet God here commands that the Lord Jesus Christ should be worshiped by the angels.

The term "firstborn" may mean first in point of time (Luke 2:7) or first in rank or honor (Psalm 89:27). It has the latter meaning here and in Romans 8:29; Colossians 1:15,18.

1:7. By way of contrast with His pre-eminent Son, God makes His angels winds and His ministers a flame of fire. He is the Creator and Director of angels. They obey His will with the speed of wind and with the fervency of fire.

1:8. Now follows a galaxy of glories in which the Lord Jesus is seen to be incomparable. First He is addressed by God as God. In Psalm 45:6 (AV) God the Father hails the Messiah with the words, "Thy throne, O God, is for ever and ever." Here again the deity of Christ is unmistakable, and the argument is all the more compelling since the proof comes from the Hebrew Scriptures. (There is at least one quotation from the Old Testament in every chapter of this letter.)

He is also the eternal Sovereign; His throne is for ever and ever. His kingdom shall indeed spread from shore to shore "till moon shall wax and wane no more."

He is the righteous King. The Psalmist speaks of Him as wielding a righteous scepter, which is a poetic way of saying that this King rules in absolute honesty and integrity.

1:9. His personal uprightness is evident from the fact that He has consistently loved righteousness and hated lawlessness. This doubtless refers primarily to His thirty-three years of life on earth, during which the eye of

God could find no flaw in His character and no failure in His conduct. He proved His fitness to reign.

Because of this personal excellence, God has anointed Him with the oil of gladness above His fellows. This means that He has given Christ the place of supremacy above all other beings. The oil here may typify the Holy Spirit; Christ was endued with the Spirit above all others (John 3:34 AV). His fellows include all those with whom He associated Himself, but the expression does not mean that they were His equals. Possibly it includes the angels, but more probably it refers to His Jewish brethren.

1:10. The Lord Jesus is the Creator of Heaven and of earth. This is demonstrated from Psalm 102:25-27. In that Psalm, the Messiah prays, "O My God . . . take Me not hence" (verse 24). This prayer at Gethsemane and Calvary is answered by God the Father, "Of old Thou didst lay the foundation of the earth, and the heavens are the work of Thy hands."

It should be noticed that God here addresses His Son as Lord, that is Jehovah. The conclusion is inescapable: the Jesus of the New Testament is the Jehovah of the Old.

1:11. In verses 11 and 12 the creation's transience is contrasted with the Creator's perpetuity. His works will perish but He Himself remains. Though the sun, moon, and stars; the mountains, the oceans, and rivers appear to be enduring, the truth is that they have built-in obsolescence. The Psalmist likens them to a garment: first, it becomes worn out; then it is folded up as unusable; then it is exchanged for something better.

1:12. Look out upon a range of snow-capped mountains, upon a glorious sunset, upon a star-studded sky. Then hear the majestic cadence of these words, "like a mantle Thou wilt roll them up, and they will be changed. But Thou art the same, and Thy years will never end." The peerless Lord Jesus is changeless and endless.

1:13. A further quotation from the Old Testament (Psalm 110:1) proves the Son's superiority. In that Psalm God invites the Messiah, "Sit at My right hand, till I make Your enemies Your footstool." The question is asked, "To what angel did God ever say anything like that?" The answer is, of course, to none.

To be seated at the right hand of God signifies a position of highest honor and limitless power. To have all one's enemies as a stool for the feet signifies universal subjugation and universal dominion.

1:14. The mission of the angels is not to rule but to serve. They are spirit beings whom God has created to minister to those who are to obtain salvation. This may be understood in two ways: first, angels minister to those who are not yet converted; or, secondly, they serve those who are saved from the penalty and power of sin but not yet saved from the presence of sin, that is, those believers who are still on earth.

Does this mean, then, that there are "guardian angels"? Why should we be surprised at such a truth? It is certain that there are evil spirits who wage unceasing conflict against God's elect (Ephesians 6:12). Is it to be wondered at that there should be holy angels who watch over those who are called to salvation?

But we must go back to the main point of the passage — not the mere existence of guardian angels but the fact that angels are inferior to the Son of God just as servants are inferior to the Universal Sovereign.

CHAPTER 2

II. *Christ Superior to the Angels* (1:4—2:18) *continued*
B. *First warning — the danger of drifting* (2:1-4)
1. *An impelling obligation*
a. *A message to hear:* Therefore we must pay the closer attention to what we have heard,
b. *A peril to fear:* lest we drift away from it.
2. *A telling proposition*
a. *The law's validity:* For if the message declared by angels was valid
b. *Its certain penalty:* and every transgression or disobedience received a just retribution,
3. *A compelling conclusion*
a. *The inescapable question:* how shall we escape if we neglect such a great salvation?
b. *The incomparable salvation*
(1) *Original declaration:* It was declared at first by the Lord,
(2) *Apostolic attestation:* and it was attested to us by those who heard Him,
(3) *Divine confirmation:* while God also bore witness by signs and wonders and various miracles and by gifts of the Holy Spirit distributed according to His own will.

27

2:1. The writer has just completed his argument that Christ is supremely better than the angels because He is the Son of God. Before showing that He is also superior as Son of Man, he pauses to inject the first of several solemn warnings that are found in the Epistle. This is a warning against drifting away from the message of the gospel.

Because of the greatness of the Giver and because of the greatness of His gift, those who hear the gospel must give the more serious attention to it. There is always the danger of drifting away from the Person and slipping back into a religion of pictures. This means drifting into apostasy — the sin for which there is no repentance.

2:2. We have already mentioned that the Jews attached special importance to the ministry of angels in their history. Perhaps the leading instance of this was in the giving of the law when myriads of angelic beings were present (Deuteronomy 33:2; Psalm 68:17).

It is true that the law was declared by angels. It is true that it was valid. It is true that every infraction was punished accordingly. These things are freely admitted.

2:3. But now the argument moves from the lesser to the greater. If those who broke the law were punished, what will be the fate of those who neglect the gospel? The law tells men what they must do; the gospel tells men what God has done. By the law is the knowledge of sin; by the gospel is the knowledge of salvation.

To neglect such a great salvation is more serious than to transgress the law. The law was given by God through angels, to Moses and then to the people. But the gospel was spoken directly by the Lord Jesus Himself. Not only so, it was confirmed to the early Christians by the apostles and by others who heard the Saviour.

2:4. God Himself authenticated the message by signs, wonders, miracles, and gifts of the Holy Spirit. Signs were those miracles of the Lord and of the apostles which signified spiritual truths. For example, the feeding of the five thousand (John 6:1-14) formed the basis of the discourse on the Bread of Life which followed (John 6:25-59). Wonders were miracles which were intended to arouse amazement in the spectators; the raising of Lazarus illustrates this (John 11:1-44). Miracles were any displays of supernatural power which contravened the laws of nature. Gifts of the Holy Spirit were special enablements given to men to speak and act in a manner that was completely beyond their natural abilities.

The purpose of all these miracles was to attest to the truth of the gospel, especially to the Jewish people, who traditionally asked for some sign before they would believe. There is some evidence that the need for confirmatory miracles ceased when the New Testament became available in written form. But it is impossible to prove conclusively that the Holy Spirit does not duplicate these miracles in other ages.

The last phrase of verse 4, "distributed according to His own will," indicates that these miraculous powers are given out by the Holy Spirit as He chooses. They are sovereign gifts of God. They cannot be demanded by men, or claimed in answer to prayer, because God has never promised them to all.

C. *His superiority as the Son of Man* (2:5-18)

1. *Dominion withheld from angels* (2:5): For it was not to angels that God subjected the world to come, of which we are speaking.

2. *Dominion assigned to man* (2:6-8b)

   a. *Insignificant:* It has been testified somewhere, "What is man

   b. *Yet remembered:* that Thou art mindful of him,

   c. *Unimportant:* or the son of man,

   d. *Yet regarded:* that Thou carest for him?

   e. *Humbled:* Thou didst make him for a little while lower than the angels,

   f. *Yet honored:* Thou hast crowned him with glory and honor,

      (1) *Complete subjection:* putting everything in subjection under his feet."

      (2) *Without exception:* Now in putting everything in subjection to man, He left nothing outside his control.

3. *Dominion lost by man* (2:8c): As it is, we do not yet see everything in subjection to him.

4. *Dominion regained by Jesus* (2:9): But we see Jesus,

   a. *Incarnation:* who for a little while was made lower than the angels,

   b. *Exaltation:* crowned with glory and honor

      (1) *Basis:* because of the suffering of death,

      (2) *Benefit:* so that by the grace of God He might taste death for every one.

5. *Dominion reached through humiliation* (2:10)
   a. *The Planner:* For it was fitting that He,
      (1) *Object:* for whom . . . [all things exist],
      (2) *Originator:* and by whom all things exist,
   b. *The purpose:* in bringing many sons to glory,
   c. *The Pioneer:* should make the pioneer of their salvation perfect
   d. *The pathway:* through suffering.
6. *The perfections of Jesus' humanity* (2:11-13)
   a. *Common humanity:* For He who sanctifies and those who are sanctified have all one origin.
   b. *Common brotherhood:* That is why He is not ashamed to call them brethren, saying, "I will proclaim Thy name to My brethren,
   c. *Common worship:* in the midst of the congregation I will praise Thee."
   d. *Common trust:* And again, "I will put My trust in Him."
   e. *Common family:* And again, "Here am I, and the children God has given Me."
7. *The blessings that flow from the humiliation* (2:14-18)
   a. *Destruction of the foe*
      (1) *His charges:* Since therefore the children share in flesh and blood,

        (2) *His cradle:* He Himself likewise partook of the same nature,

        (3) *His cross:* that through death

        (4) *His conquest:* He might destroy him who has the power of death, that is, the devil.

   b. *Emancipation from fear*

        (1) *The liberated slaves:* and deliver all those who through fear of death

        (2) *Their lifelong servitude:* were subject to lifelong bondage.

   c. *Expiation for sin*

        (1) *The cause He espoused*

           (a) *Not angelic:* For surely it is not with angels that He is concerned

           (b) *But Abrahamic:* but with the descendants of Abraham.

        (2) *The nature He assumed:* Therefore He had to be made like His brethren in every respect,

        (3) *The office He filled:* so that He might become a merciful and faithful high priest in the service of God,

        (4) *The result He accomplished:* to make expiation for the sins of the people.

   d. *Help for the tempted*

        (1) *Acquainted with suffering:* For because He Himself has suffered and been tempted,

        (2) *Able to succor:* He is able to help those who are tempted.

2:5. In the first chapter we saw that Christ is superior to the angels as the Son of God. Now it will be shown that He is also superior as the Son of Man. It will help us in following the flow of thought if we remember that, to the Jewish mind, the thought of Christ's incarnation was incredible and the fact of His humiliation was shameful. To the Jews, Jesus was a man and only a man, and therefore He belonged to a lower order than the angels. The following verses show that even as Man, Jesus was better than the angels.

First, it is pointed out that God did not decree that the habitable world of the future should be under the control of angels. The world of the future here means the golden age of peace and prosperity which the prophets so frequently mentioned. We speak of it as the millennium.

2:6. Psalm 8:4-6 is quoted to show that the eventual dominion over the earth has been given to man, not to angels. In a sense, man is insignificant, and yet God is mindful of him. In a sense, man is unimportant, yet God cares for him.

2:7. In the scale of creation, man has been given a lower place than the angels. He is more limited as to knowledge, mobility, and power. And he is subject to death. Yet in the purposes of God, man is destined to be crowned with glory and honor. The limitations of his body and mind will be largely removed, and he will be exalted on the earth.

2:8. Everything will be put under man's authority in that coming day — the angelic hosts, the world of animals, birds and fishes, the planetary system — in fact, every part of the created universe will be put under his control.

This was God's original intention for man. He told him, for instance, to "fill the earth and subdue it; and have dominion over the fish of the sea and over the birds of the air and over every living thing that moves upon the earth" (Genesis 1:28).

Why then don't we see everything in subjection to him? The answer is that man lost his dominion because of his sin. It was Adam's sin that brought the curse on creation. Docile creatures became ferocious. The ground began to bring forth thorns and thistles. Man's control over nature was challenged and limited.

2:9. However, when the Son of Man returns to reign over the earth, man's dominion will be restored. Jesus, as Man, will restore that which Adam lost, and more besides. So while we do not see everything under man's control at the present time, we do see Jesus, and in Him we find the key to man's eventual rule over the earth.

For a little while, He was made lower than the angels, specifically, for the thirty-three years of His earthly ministry. His descent from Heaven to Bethlehem, to Gethsemane, to Gabbatha, to Golgotha, and to the tomb mark the stages in His humiliation. But now He is crowned with glory and honor. His exaltation is a result of His suffering and death; the cross led to the crown.

God's gracious purpose in it all was that Christ might taste death for every man. The Saviour died as our Representative and as our Substitute; that is, He died as man and He died for man. He bore in His body on the cross all God's judgment against sin so that those who believe on Him will never have to bear it.

2:10. It was entirely in keeping with the righteous character of God that man's dominion should be restored through the humiliation of the Saviour. Sin had disturbed God's order. Before order could be brought out of chaos, sin must be dealt with righteously. It was consistent with the holy character of God that Christ should suffer, bleed, and die to put away sin.

The wise Planner is described as the One "for whom and by whom all things exist." First He is the objective or goal of all creation; all things were made for His glory and pleasure. But He is also the Source or Originator of all creation; nothing was made apart from Him.

His great purpose was to bring many sons to glory. When we consider our own worthlessness, it staggers us to think that He would have even bothered with us, but it is because He is the God of all grace that He has called us to His eternal glory.

The cost of our glorification? The Pioneer of our salvation had to be made perfect through suffering. As far as His moral character is concerned, the Lord Jesus was always sinlessly perfect. He could never be made perfect in this respect. But He had to be made perfect *as our Saviour.* In order to purchase eternal redemption for us, He had to suffer all the punishment that our sins deserved. We could not be saved by His spotless life but only by His substitutionary death.

God found a way of saving us that was worthy of Himself. He sent His only-begotten Son to die in our place.

2:11. The next three verses emphasize the perfection of Jesus' manhood. If He is going to regain the dominion which Adam lost, then it must be demonstrated that He is true man.

First the fact is stated: "For both He that sanctifieth and they that are sanctified are all of one" (ASV), that is, they are all possessors of humanity. Or if we accept the RSV reading, ". . . have all one origin," the meaning is that in their humanity, they all have one God and Father.

Christ is the One who sanctifies, that is, He sets apart or separates men to God from the world. Blessed are all those whom He thus sets apart!

The following excerpt is quoted from the appendix of a course on Hebrews, written by the author for Moody Bible Institute, entitled, *Hebrews: From Shadow to Substance:*

In the Biblical sense, *to sanctify is to set apart or to separate.* A sanctified person or thing is one set apart from ordinary uses to be for God's own possession, use, and enjoyment.

The opposite of sanctification is profanation.

There are three types of sanctification in the Bible:

Positional sanctification means that a person or thing has been set apart by someone else, usually by God, and that the person or thing did not of necessity have an active part in the matter.

Practical sanctification, on the other hand, describes the process by which a person actively submits himself to God and separates himself from evil.

Perfect sanctification refers to the believer's ultimate condition — when he will be perfectly conformed to Christ in Heaven. He will have his glorified body and be forever free from sin (Romans 8:29-30; 1 John 3:1-3; Jude 24-25).

Positional sanctification may apply to any of the following:

1. Inanimate things such as the altar, the laver, and the vessels of the Tabernacle were sanctified (Leviticus 8:10; 1 Timothy 4:5). Also the seventh day (Genesis 2:3).

2. The Lord Jesus Christ was sanctified and sent into the world (John 10:36).

3. Unbelievers are sometimes spoken of as sanctified (1

Corinthians 7:14). This does not mean that they are in themselves holy, but simply that they have been set apart to a position of external privilege because of their relationship to true believers.

4. Believers are sanctified (1 Corinthians 1:2; 6:11).

Practical or progressive sanctification is applied particularly to believers:

1. "This is the will of God, even your sanctification" (1 Thessalonians 4:3). This means that God wants His people to live lives of purity and honor.

2. "The very God of peace sanctify you wholly" (1 Thessalonians 5:23). Paul here prays that Christians may live in practical holiness, and that this holiness may extend to every part of their being — spirit, soul, and body.

The reader should be on the lookout for the various passages in the Epistle to the Hebrews where the subject of sanctification is mentioned, and should seek to determine which of the above types of sanctification is in view.

It is because He became a true Man that He is not ashamed to speak of His followers as brothers. Is it possible that the Eternal Sovereign of the universe should become man and identify Himself so closely with His creatures that He would call them brothers?

2:12. The answer is found in Psalm 22:22 where we hear Him say, "I will tell of Thy name to My brethren." The same verse also pictures Him as identified with His people in common worship, "in the midst of the congregation I will praise Thee." In His dying agony, He looked forward to the day when He would lead the ransomed throng in praise to God the Father.

2:13. Two more verses are quoted from the Jewish Scriptures to prove Christ's humanity. In Isaiah 8:17 (Septuagint), He speaks of putting His trust in God. Implicit confidence in Jehovah is one of the greatest marks of true manhood. Then in Isaiah 8:18 (KJV), the Lord is quoted as saying, "Behold, I and the children, whom the Lord hath given Me." The thought is that they are members of a common family, acknowledging a common Father.

2:14. Those who consider the humiliation of the Son of Man to be shameful are now asked to consider four important blessings that flow from His passion.

The first is the destruction of Satan. How did this happen? There was a special sense in which God gave His children to Christ to sanctify, save, and emancipate. Since these children had human natures, the Lord Jesus assumed a body of flesh and blood. He set aside the outward display of His deity and veiled His godhead in a "robe of clay."

But He did not stop at Bethlehem. "All the way to Calvary He went for me because He loved me so."

Through His death, He destroyed the one who has the power of death, that is, the devil. Destruction here means the loss of well-being rather than loss of being. It means to nullify or to bring to naught. Satan is still actively opposing the purposes of God in the world, but he received a death wound at the cross. His time is short and his doom is sure. He is a defeated foe.

In what sense does the devil have the power of death?

Probably the chief sense in which he has this power is in *demanding* death. It was through Satan that sin first entered into the world. God's holiness decreed the death of all who sinned. In his role as adversary, the devil, therefore, can demand that the penalty be paid.

In heathen lands his power is also seen in the ability of his agents, the witch doctors, to pronounce a curse on a person and for that person to die without any natural cause.

There is no suggestion in Scripture that the devil can inflict death on a believer without the permission of God (Job 2:6), and therefore he cannot set the time of a believer's death. Through wicked men, he is sometimes permitted to kill the believer. But Jesus warned His disciples not to fear those who could destroy the body, but rather to fear God who can destroy both soul and body in hell (Matthew 10:28).

In the Old Testament, Enoch and Elijah went to Heaven without dying. No doubt this was because, as believers, they were reckoned to have died in the still-future death of Christ.

When Christ comes at the rapture, all living believers will go to Heaven without dying. But they too escape death because God's holiness was satisfied for them in the death of Christ.

The risen Christ now has "the keys of Death and Hades" (Revelation 1:18), that is, He has complete authority over them.

2:15. The second blessing traced to Christ's humiliation is emancipation from fear. Before the cross, the fear of death held men in lifelong servitude. Though there are occasional flashes of light in the Old Testament concerning life after death, the general impression is one of uncertainty, horror, and gloom. What was hazy then is clear now because Christ brought life and immortality to light by the gospel (2 Timothy 1:10).

2:16. The third tremendous blessing is expiation of sin. In coming into the world, the Lord did not espouse the cause of angels but of the seed of Abraham. This may mean Abraham's physical descendants, the Jews, or it may mean his spiritual seed — the believers of every age. The important point is that they are human, not angelic beings.

2:17. This being so, it was necessary that He should be made like His brethren in every respect. He assumed true and perfect manhood. He became subject to human desires, thoughts, feelings, emotions, and affections — with this important exception: He was without sin. His humanity was the ideal; ours has been invaded by a foreign element, sin.

His perfect humanity fits Him to be "a merciful and faithful high priest in the service of God." He can be merciful to man and faithful to God. His chief function as High Priest is to make expiation for the sins of the people. To accomplish this He did what no other high priest ever did or could do — He offered Himself as a sinless sacrifice. He willingly died in our place.

2:18. The fourth blessing is help for the tempted. Because He has suffered and has been tempted, He is able to help those who are going through temptation. Someone has aptly paraphrased this verse, "He can help others who are going through it because He has been through it Himself."

Here again we must add a word of qualification. The Lord Jesus was tempted from without, but never from within. The temptation in the wilderness shows Him being tempted from without. Satan appeared to Him and sought to appeal to Him by external stimuli. But the Saviour could never be tempted to sin by lusts and passions within Himself, for there was no sin in Him and nothing to respond to sin.

CHAPTER 3

III. *Christ Superior to Moses* (3:1—4:13)
  A. *Introductory appeal* (3:1)
    1. *Its objects:* Therefore, holy brethren, who share in a heavenly call,
    2. *Its Subject:* consider Jesus, the apostle and high priest of our confession.
  B. *Admitted similarity* (3:2): He was faithful to Him who appointed Him, just as Moses also was faithful in God's house.
  C. *Acknowledged superiority* (3:3-6a)
    1. *Greater as Builder*
      a. *The fact of superiority:* Yet Jesus has been counted worthy of as much more glory than Moses
      b. *The degree of superiority:* as the builder of a house has more honor than the house.
    2. *Greater as God*
      a. *Basic necessity:* (For every house is built by some one,
      b. *Divine reality:* but the builder of all things is God.)
    3. *Greater as Son*
      a. *Moses, a servant:* Now Moses was faithful in all God's house as a servant, to

testify to the things that were to be
spoken later,

b. *Christ, a Son:* but Christ was faithful
over God's house as a son.

D. *Added reminder* (3:6b)

1. *Our privileged position:* And we are His
house

2. *Our prescribed practice:* if indeed we hold
fast the boldness and the boast of hope firm
to the end (JND).

3:1. Moses was one of Israel's greatest national
heroes. Therefore the third main step in the writer's
strategy is to demonstrate Christ's infinite superiority to
Moses.

The message is addressed to "holy brethren, who
share in a heavenly call." All true believers are holy as to
their position, and they should be holy as to their
practice. In Christ they are holy; in themselves they
ought to be holy.

Their heavenly call is in contrast to the earthly call of
Israel. Old Testament saints were called to material
blessings in the land of promise (though they did have a
heavenly hope as well). In the Church age, believers are
called to spiritual blessings in the heavenlies now and to
a heavenly inheritance in the future.

"Consider Jesus." He is eminently worthy of our
consideration as the Apostle and High Priest of our
confession. In confessing Him as Apostle, we mean that
He represents God to us. In confessing Him as High
Priest, we mean that He represents us before God.

3:2. There is one aspect in which He was admittedly similar to Moses. He was faithful to God, just as Moses was faithful in God's house. The house here does not mean only the Tabernacle but also the entire sphere in which Moses represented God's interests. It is the house of Israel, God's chosen earthly people.

3:3. But there the similarity ends. In every other respect there is undisputed superiority. First the Lord Jesus is worthy of more honor than the patriarch because the builder of a house has more honor than the house itself. The Lord Jesus was the builder of God's house; Moses was a part of the house.

3:4. Secondly, Jesus is greater because He is God. Every house must have a builder. The One who built all things is God. From John 1:3, Colossians 1:16, and Hebrews 1:2,10, we learn that the Lord Jesus was the active agent in creation. The conclusion is unavoidable — Jesus Christ is God.

3:5. The third point is that Christ is greater as Son. Moses was a faithful servant in all God's house (Numbers 12:7 AV), pointing men forward to the coming Messiah. He testified "to the things that were to be spoken later," that is, the good news of salvation in Christ. That is why Jesus said on one occasion, "If you believed Moses, you would believe Me, for he wrote of Me" (John 5:46). In His discourse with the disciples on the road to Emmaus, Jesus began at Moses and all the prophets, and "interpreted to them in all the scriptures the things concerning Himself" (Luke 24:27).

3:6. But Christ was faithful over God's house as a Son, not a servant, and in His case, sonship means equality with God. God's house is His house (ASV).

Here the writer explains what is meant by God's house today. It is composed of all true believers in the Lord Jesus: "We are His house if we hold fast our confidence and pride in our hope." At first this might seem to imply that our salvation is dependent on our holding fast. In that case, salvation would be by our endurance rather than by Christ's finished work on the cross. The true meaning is that we prove we are God's house if we hold fast. Endurance is a proof of reality. Those who lose confidence in Christ and in His promises and return to rituals and ceremonies show that they were never born again. It is against such apostasy that the following warning is directed.

III. *Christ Superior to Moses* (3:1—4:13) *(continued)*
    E. *Second warning — the danger of hardening the heart* (3:7—4:13)
        1. *The Spirit's admonition* (3:7-11): Therefore, as the Holy Spirit says,
            a. *Present occasion:* "Today,
            b. *Divine instruction:* when you hear His voice,
            c. *Improper reaction:* do not harden your hearts
            d. *Historical illustration:* as in the rebellion,
               (1) *The desert:* on the day of testing in the wilderness,
               (2) *The deed:* where your fathers put Me to the test

      (3) *The duration:* and saw My works for forty years.

      (4) *The displeasure:* Therefore I was provoked with that generation,

      (5) *The denunciation:* and said, 'They always go astray in their hearts; they have not known My ways.'

      (6) *The decision:* As I swore in My wrath, 'They shall never enter My rest.' "

2. *The personal application* (3:12-15)

   a. *The unbelieving heart:* Take care, brethren, lest there be in any of you an evil, unbelieving heart, leading you to fall away from the living God.

   b. *The hardened heart*

      (1) *Helpful exhorting:* But exhort one another every day, as long as it is called "today,"

      (2) *Sinful hardening:* that none of you may be hardened by the deceitfulness of sin.

      (3) *Needful persevering:* For we share in Christ, if only we hold our first confidence firm to the end,

      (4) *Heedful hearing:* while it is said, "Today, when you hear His voice, do not harden your hearts as in the rebellion."

3. *The historical interpretation* (3:16-19)

    a. *Rebellion:* Who were they that heard and yet were rebellious? Was it not all those who left Egypt under the leadership of Moses?

    b. *Provocation:* And with whom was He provoked forty years? Was it not with those who sinned, whose bodies fell in the wilderness?

    c. *Retribution:* And to whom did He swear that they should never enter His rest, but to those who were disobedient?

    d. *Conclusion:* So we see that they were unable to enter because of unbelief.

3:7. At this point the writer interjects the second main warning of the Epistle — a warning against hardening the heart. It had happened to Israel in the wilderness and it could happen again. So the Holy Spirit is still speaking through Psalm 95:7-11, as He did when He first inspired it, "O that today you would harken to His voice!"

3:8. Whenever God speaks, we should be swift to hear. To doubt His Word is to call Him a liar and to incur His wrath.

Yet that was Israel's history in the wilderness. It was a dreary record of complaint, lust, idolatry, unbelief, and rebellion. At Rephidim, for instance, they complained because of lack of water and doubted God's presence in their midst (Exodus 17:1-7). And at the wilderness of Paran when the unbelieving spies returned with an evil report of discouragement and doubt (Numbers 13:25-29), the people decided that they should go back to Egypt, the land of their bondage (Numbers 14:4).

3:9. God was so highly incensed that He decreed that the people should wander in the wilderness for forty years (Numbers 14:33-34). Of all those who came out of Egypt who were twenty years old or older, only two would ever enter the land of Canaan — Caleb and Joshua (Numbers 14:28-30).

It is significant that just as Israel spent forty years in the wilderness, so the Spirit of God dealt with the nation of Israel for approximately forty years after the death of Christ. The nation hardened its heart against the message of Christ. In A.D. 70, Jerusalem was destroyed and the people were scattered among the Gentile nations.

3:10. God's keen displeasure with Israel in the wilderness brought forth this stern denunciation. He accused them of a perpetual proneness to wander away from Him, and of a willful ignorance of His ways.

3:11. In His wrath, He swore that they would never enter into His rest, that is, into the land of Canaan.

3:12. In verses 12-15, we have the application which the Holy Spirit draws for us from Israel's experience. As elsewhere in the Epistle, the readers are addressed as brethren. This does not mean that they were all true Christians. They professed to be genuinely converted, but there was always the possibility that some were only nominal Christians. So all who profess to be believers should be constantly on guard against a pernicious,

48 *The Epistle to the Hebrews*

unbelieving heart that might cause them to fall away from the living God. It is a constant menace.

3:13. One antidote is mutual exhortation. Especially in days of difficulty and distress, God's people should be constantly urging others not to forsake Christ for religions that cannot deal with sin effectively.

Notice that this exhortation is not limited to a ministerial class but is the duty of all brethren. It should continue as long as it is called "today," that is, as long as God's offer of salvation by grace through faith continues. "Today" is the accepted time; it is the day of salvation.

To fall away is to be hardened by the deceitfulness of sin. Sin often looks beautiful in anticipation. Here it offers escape from the reproach of Christ, lower standards of holiness, rituals that appeal to the aesthetic senses, and the promise of earthly gain. But it is hideous in retrospect. It leaves a man with no forgiveness of sins, no hope beyond the grave, and no possibility of repentance.

3:14. Again we are reminded that we have become companions of Christ if we hold fast our first confidence steadfast to the end. Verses like this are often used to show that a person can be saved and then lost again. However, such an interpretation is impossible because the overwhelming testimony of the Bible is that salvation is freely bestowed by God's grace, purchased by Christ's blood, received by man's faith, and evidenced by his good works. True faith always has the quality of permanence. We don't hold fast in order to retain our salvation, but as proof that we have been genuinely saved. Faith is the root of salvation; endurance is the fruit. Who are Christ's companions? The answer is, "Those who by their steadfastness in the faith prove that they really belong to Him."

3:15. Now the writer concludes the personal application of Israel's sad experience by repeating the words of Psalm 95:7-8: "O that today you would hearken to His voice! Harden not your hearts, as at Meribah, as on the day at Massah in the wilderness." This poignant appeal, once directed to Israel, is now directed to any who might be tempted to forsake the good news and return to the law.

3:16. The chapter closes with a historical interpretation of Israel's apostasy. In a series of three questions and answers, the writer traces Israel's rebellion, provocation, and retribution. Then he states the conclusion.

Rebellion. The rebels are identified as all those who left Egypt under the leadership of Moses. Caleb and Joshua were the lone exceptions.

3:17. *Provocation.* It was these same rebels who provoked Jehovah for forty years. There were about 600,000 of them, and by the time the forty years were ended, the desert was dotted with about 600,000 graves.

3:18. *Retribution.* These were the same ones who were excluded from the land of Canaan because of their disobedience.

The simple recital of these questions and answers should have a profound influence on any who might be tempted to leave the despised minority of true Christians for the vast majority who have an outward form of religion but deny the power of godliness. Is the majority always right? In this chapter of Israel's history, only two were right and over half a million were wrong.

A. T. Pierson emphasizes the seriousness of Israel's sin as follows:

Their unbelief was a fourfold provocation:

1. It was an assault on God's truth, and made Him a liar.
2. It was an assault upon His power, for it counted Him as weak and unable to bring them in.
3. It was an attack upon His immutability; for, although they did not say so, their course implied that He was a changeable God, and could not do the wonders He had once wrought.
4. It was also an attack upon His fatherly faithfulness, as though He would encourage an expectation He had no intention of fulfilling.

On the contrary, Caleb and Joshua honored God by accounting His word absolutely true, His power infinite, His disposition unchangingly gracious, and His faithfulness such that He would never awaken any hope which He would not bring to fruition.

3:19. *Conclusion.* It was unbelief that kept the rebellious children out of the promised land, and it is unbelief that keeps man out of God's inheritance in every dispensation. The moral is clear: beware of an evil heart of unbelief.

CHAPTER 4

III. *Christ Superior to Moses* (3:1–4:13) *(continued)*

   E. *Second warning – the danger of hardening the heart* (3:7–4:13) (continued)

      4. *The urgent exhortation* (4:1-13)

         a. *Rest provided:* Therefore, while the promise of entering His rest remains,

         b. *Relapse possible:* let us fear lest any of you be judged to have failed to reach it.

         c. *Rest preached*

            (1) *Recipients:* For good news came to us just as to them;

            (2) *Result:* but the message which they heard did not benefit them,

            (3) *Reason:* because it did not meet with faith in the hearers.

         d. *Rest procurable*

            (1) *Attained by faith:* For we who have believed enter that rest,

            (2) *Forfeited by unbelief:* as He has said, "As I swore in My wrath, 'They shall never enter My rest,' "

            (3) *Distinct from creation rest:* although His works were finished from the foundation of the world. For He has somewhere spoken of the seventh

day in this way, "And God rested on the seventh day from all His works."

(4) *Subsequent to creation rest:* And again in this place He said, "They shall never enter My rest."

(5) *Available still*

   (a) *Possession intended:* Since therefore it remains for some to enter it,

   (b) *Prior offer forfeited:* and those who formerly received the good news failed to enter because of disobedience,

   (c) *Promise later repeated:* again He sets a certain day, "Today," saying through David so long afterward, in the words already quoted, "Today, when you hear His voice, do not harden your hearts."

      i. *If rest obtained:* For if Joshua had given them rest,

      ii. *Renewed offer unnecessary:* God would not speak later of another day.

   (d) *Promise still standing:* So then, there remains a sabbath rest for the people of God;

      i. *Definition:* for whoever enters God's rest also ceases from his labors

        ii. *Illustration:* as God did from His.

e. *Resolution prescribed*

  (1) *Diligence desirable:* Let us therefore strive to enter that rest,

  (2) *Downfall preventable:* that no man fall by the same sort of disobedience.

  (3) *Detection inevitable:*

    (a) *The Word of God:* For the word of God is

      i. *Living:* living

      ii. *Energizing:* and active,

      iii. *Cutting:* sharper than any two-edged sword,

      iv. *Dividing:* piercing to the division of soul and spirit, of joints and marrow,

      v. *Discerning:* and discerning the thoughts and intentions of the heart.

    (b) *The omniscient Lord*

      i. *Nothing concealed:* And before Him no creature is hidden,

      ii. *Everything revealed:* but all are open and laid bare to the eyes of Him with whom we have to do.

The following verses form one of the most difficult passages in the entire letter. There is little agreement among the commentators as to the exact flow of the argument, although the over-all teaching of the section is fairly clear.

The theme of 4:1-13 is God's rest and the need for diligence in reaching it. It will be helpful for us at the outset if we notice that several kinds of rest are mentioned in the Bible:

1. God rested after the sixth day of creation (Genesis 2:2). This rest did not indicate weariness as a result of toil, but rather satisfaction with the work that had been completed. It was the rest of complacency (Genesis 1:31). God's rest was interrupted by the entrance of sin into the world. Since that time He has been working ceaselessly, as Jesus said, "My Father is working still, and I am working" (John 5:17).

2. Canaan was intended to be a land of rest for the children of Israel. Most of them never entered the land, and those who did, failed to find the rest that God intended for them. Canaan is used here as a type or picture of God's final, eternal rest. Many of those who failed to reach Canaan (Korah, Dathan, and Abiram, for example) picture present-day apostates who fail to reach God's rest because of their unbelief.

3. Believers today enjoy rest of conscience, knowing that the penalty for their sins has been paid through the finished work of the Lord Jesus. This is the rest which the Saviour promised, "Come to Me ... and I will give you rest" (Matthew 11:28).

4. The believer also enjoys a rest in serving the Lord. Whereas the preceding is a rest of salvation, this is a rest of service. "Take My yoke upon you, and learn from Me . . . and you will find rest for your souls" (Matthew 11:29).

5. Then finally there is the eternal rest which awaits the believer in the Father's house in Heaven. This future rest, also called a sabbath rest (Hebrews 4:9), is the final rest of which the others are either types or foretastes. This rest is the principal subject of Hebrews 4:1-13.

4:1. No one needs to think that the promise of rest is no longer valid. It has never had a complete and final fulfillment in the past; therefore the offer is still in effect.

But all who profess to be believers should make sure that they do not fall short of the goal. If their profession is empty, there is always the danger of turning away from Christ and embracing some religious system that is powerless to save.

4:2. We have had good news preached to us — the good news of eternal life through faith in Christ. The Israelites also had good news preached to them — the good news of rest in the land of Canaan. But they did not benefit from the gospel of rest.

There are two possible explanations for their failure, depending on which translation of verse 2 we adopt. According to the RSV, the reason for their failure was that the message "did not meet with faith in the hearers." In other words, they did not believe it or act upon it.

The other explanation is that "they were not united by faith with them that heard" (ASV margin). The meaning here is that the majority of the Israelites were not united by faith with Caleb and Joshua, the two spies who believed the promise of God.

In either case, the prominent idea is that unbelief excluded them from the rest which God had prepared for them in the land of promise.

4:3. The continuity of thought becomes very obscure in this verse. There seem to be three disjointed and unrelated clauses, yet we can see that there is a common thread in each clause — the theme of God's rest.

First we learn that we who believe are the ones who enter God's rest. Faith is the key that opens the door. As has been pointed out already, believers today enjoy rest of conscience because they know that they will never be brought into judgment for their sins (John 5:24). But it is also true that those who believe are the only ones who will ever enter God's final rest in glory. It is probably this future rest that is primarily intended here.

The next clause reinforces the idea by stating it negatively: "As He has said, 'As I swore in My wrath, They shall never enter My rest'" (quoted from Psalm 95:11). Just as faith admits, so unbelief excludes. We who trust Christ are sure of God's rest; the unbelieving Israelites could not be sure of it because they did not believe God's Word.

The third clause presents the most difficulty: it says, "Although His works were finished from the foundation of the world." Perhaps the simplest explanation is found by linking this with the preceding clause. There God had used the future tense in speaking of His rest: "They shall never enter My rest." The future tense implies that God's rest is still a live option, even though some forfeited it through disobedience, and this rest is still available in spite of the fact that God's works were "finished from the foundation of the world."

4:4. This verse is intended to prove from Scripture that God rested after the work of creation was completed. The author's vagueness in identifying the passage quoted does not indicate any ignorance on his part. It is merely a literary device in quoting a verse from a Book that was not at that time divided into chapters and verses. The verse is adapted from Genesis 2:2: "And God rested on the seventh day from all His works."

Here the *past* tense is used and it might seem to indicate to some that God's rest belongs only to history and not to prophecy, that it has no relevance for us today. But that is not the case.

4:5. To reinforce the idea that the reference to God's rest after creation does not mean that it is a closed issue, the writer again quotes with slight change from Psalm 95:11, where the *future* tense is used, "They shall never enter My rest." He is saying, in effect, in your thinking, don't confine God's rest to what happened back in Genesis 2; remember that God later spoke about His rest as something that was still available.

4:6. Up to this point in the argument we have seen that, from the creation, God has been offering rest to mankind. The admission gate has been open.

The Israelites in the wilderness failed to enter because

of their disobedience. But that did not mean that the promise was no longer in effect!

4:7. The next step is to show that even in the days of David, about 500 years after the Israelites were shut out from Canaan, God was still using the word "today" as a day of opportunity. The writer had already quoted Psalm 95:7-8 in Hebrews 3:7,8,15. He now quotes it again to prove that God's promise of rest did not cease with the Israelites in the wilderness. In David's time, He was still pleading with men to trust Him and not to harden their hearts.

4:8. Some Israelites did, of course, enter Canaan with Joshua (those who were under twenty when they left Egypt). But even these did not enjoy the final rest which God has prepared for those who love Him. There was conflict in Canaan, and sin, sickness, sorrow, suffering, and death.

If they had exhausted God's promise of rest, then He would not have offered it again in the time of David.

4:9. The preceding verses have been leading up to this conclusion: "So then, there remains a sabbath rest for the people of God." Here the writer uses a different word for rest, one which is correctly translated sabbath rest in the RSV. It refers to the eternal rest which will be enjoyed by all who have been redeemed by the precious blood of Christ. It is a sabbath keeping that will never end.

4:10. Whoever enters God's rest enjoys a cessation from labor, just as God did on the seventh day.

Before we were saved, we sought to work for our salvation. When we realized that Christ had finished the work at Calvary, we abandoned our own worthless efforts and trusted the risen Redeemer.

After salvation, we expend ourselves in loving toil for the One who loved us and gave Himself for us. Our good works are the fruit of the indwelling Holy Spirit. Oftentimes we are weary in His service though not weary of it.

In God's eternal rest, we shall cease from our labors down here. This does not mean that we will be inactive in Heaven. We shall still worship and serve Him, but then there will be no fatigue, distress, persecution, or affliction.

4:11. The previous verses demonstrate that God's rest is still available. This verse says that diligence is necessary in order to enter that rest. The suggestion that we should "labour" for it (AV) misses the point. We must be diligent to make sure that our one and only hope is Jesus Christ, the Lord. We must diligently resist any temptation to profess faith in Him and then to renounce Him in the heat of suffering and persecution.

The Israelites were careless. They treated God's promises lightly. They hankered for Egypt, the land of their bondage. They were not diligent in appropriating God's promises by faith. As a result, they never reached Canaan. We should be warned by their example.

4:12. The next two verses contain a solemn warning that unbelief never goes undetected. It is detected first by the Word of God. This may mean the living Word, Jesus Christ, or the written Word, the Bible. There is a mysterious, marvelous, inexplicable relationship between the two, and all that is said here is true of them both. The Word of God is:

> living — constantly and actively alive
>
> active — energizing
>
> cutting — sharper than any two-edged sword
>
> dividing — piercing the soul and piercing the spirit, the two invisible, nonmaterial parts of man. Piercing the joints and piercing the marrow, the joints permitting the outward movements and the marrow being the hidden but vital life of the bones.
>
> discerning — discriminating and judging with regard to the thoughts and intentions of the heart.

4:13. Secondly, unbelief is detected by the living Lord. Here the pronoun shifts from the impersonal to the personal: "And before *Him* no creature is hidden." Nothing escapes His notice. He is absolutely omniscient. He is constantly aware of all that is going on in the universe. Of course the important point in the context is that He knows where there is real faith and where there is only an intellectual assent to facts.

IV. *Christ's High Priesthood Superior to Aaron's* (4:14—7:28)

    A. *Introductory appeals* (4:14-16)

        1. *His personal excellence*

            a. *A great High Priest:* Since then we have a great high priest

            b. *Exalted in Heaven:* who has passed through the heavens,

            c. *Human:* Jesus,

d. *Divine:* the Son of God,
2. *Consequent exhortation:* let us hold fast our confession.
3. *His personal experience*
    a. *Capably sympathetic:* For we have not a high priest who is unable to sympathize with our weaknesses,
    b. *Thoroughly tested:* but one who in every respect has been tempted as we are,
    c. *Sinlessly perfect:* yet without sinning.
4. *Consequent invitation*
    a. *Manner:* Let us then with confidence
    b. *Action:* draw near
    c. *Place:* to the throne of grace,
    d. *Purpose:* that we may receive mercy and find grace to help
    e. *Occasion:* in time of need.

4:14. These verses take up again the strong current of the writer's thought which he had introduced in 3:1 — Christ as the great High Priest of His people. They present Him as the great resource of His needy people, able to keep them from falling. Also they change the emphasis "from the Word as scrutinizer to the Lord as Sympathizer."

Notice the excellencies of our wonderful Lord:

1. He is a great High Priest. There were many high priests under the Mosaic economy, but none was ever called great.
2. He has passed through the atmospheric heaven and the stellar heaven to the third Heaven, the

dwelling place of God. This speaks, of course, of His ascension and glorification at the Father's right hand.

3. He is human. Jesus was the name given to Him at His birth and it is the name that is particularly linked with His humanity.

4. He is divine. The Son of God, when used of Christ, speaks of His absolute equality with God the Father. His humanity qualified Him from our viewpoint; His deity from God's viewpoint. No wonder He is called a great High Priest.

4:15. Then too we must consider His experience. No one can truly sympathize with someone else unless he has been through the same experience himself. As Man our Lord has shared our experiences and can therefore understand the testings which we endure.

> In every pang that rends the heart,
> The Man of Sorrows has a part.

He was tempted in every respect as we are, yet without sin. The Scriptures guard the sinless perfection of the Lord Jesus with jealous care, and we should too. He knew no sin (2 Corinthians 5:21), He committed no sin (1 Peter 2:22), and there is no sin in Him (1 John 3:5).

It was impossible for Him to sin, either as God or as Man. As the perfect Man, He could do nothing of His own accord; He was absolutely obedient to the Father (John 5:19), and certainly the Father would never lead Him to sin.

To argue that His temptation was not meaningful if He could not sin is fallacious. One purpose of the temptation was to demonstrate conclusively that He could not sin.

I. M. Haldeman has pointed out that if you put gold to the test, the test is not less valid because the gold is pure. If there was impurity, the test would show it up. Similarly it is wrong to argue that if He could not sin, He was not perfectly human. Sin is not an essential element in humanity; rather it is a foreign intruder. Our humanity has been marred by sin; His is perfect humanity.

If Jesus could have sinned as a Man on earth, what is to prevent His sinning as a Man in Heaven? He did not leave His humanity behind when He ascended to the Father's right hand. He was impeccable on earth and He is impeccable in Heaven.

4:16. Now the gracious invitation is extended: draw near with confidence to the throne of grace. Our confidence is based on the knowledge that He died to save us and that He lives to keep us. We are assured of a hearty welcome because He has told us to come.

The people in Old Testament days could not draw near to Him. Only the high priest could approach Him, and then on only one day of the year. We can go into His presence at any time of the day or night and obtain mercy and grace to help in time of need. His mercy covers the things we should not have done, and His grace empowers us to do what we should do but do not have the power to do.

"I am never tired of pointing out that the Greek

phrase translated 'in time of need' is a colloquialism of which 'in the nick of time' is the exact equivalent. 'That we may receive mercy and find grace to help *in the nick of time'* — grace just when and where I need it. You are attacked by temptation. At the moment of assault, you look to Him, and the grace is there to help in the nick of time. There is no postponement of your petition until the evening hour of prayer. But there in the city street with the flaming temptation in front of you, turn to Christ with a cry for help, and the grace will be there in the nick of time" (G. Campbell Morgan).

CHAPTER 5

IV. *Christ's High Priesthood Superior to Aaron's* (4:14–7:28) *(continued)*
  B. *Description of the Aaronic priest* (5:1-4)
    1. *Selected from among men:* For every high priest chosen from among men
    2. *Serves on behalf of men*: is appointed to act on behalf of men
      a. *In relation to God:* in relation to God,
      b. *In connection with sins:* to offer gifts and sacrifices for sins.
    3. *Sympathizes with human frailty:* He can deal gently with the ignorant and wayward, since he himself is beset with weakness.
    4. *Sacrifices for himself:* Because of this he is bound to offer sacrifice for his own sins
    5. *Sacrifices for the people:* as well as for those of the people.
    6. *Scorns self-appointment:* And one does not take the honor upon himself,
      a. *Selection:* but he is called by God,
      b. *Illustration:* just as Aaron was.
  C. *Christ's fitness as a high priest* (5:5-10)
    1. *Appointment:* So also Christ did not exalt Himself to be made a high priest,

    a. *Better source:* but was appointed by Him [God] who said to Him,

    b. *Better relationship:* "Thou art My Son, today I have begotten Thee";

    c. *Better order:* as He says also in another place, "Thou art a priest for ever, after the order of Melchizedek."

2. *Actual humanity*

    a. *His prayers:* In the days of His flesh, Jesus offered up prayers and supplications,

    b. *His tears:* with loud cries and tears,

    c. *His trust:* to Him who was able to save Him out of death (JND),

    d. *His answers:* and He was heard for His godly fear.

3. *Acquired qualification*

    a. *Divine relation:* Son though He was (Con),

    b. *Experiential instruction:* He learned obedience through what He suffered;

    c. *Official perfection:* and being made perfect

    d. *Earned distinction:* He became the source of eternal salvation to all who obey Him,

    e. *Sovereign designation:* being designated by God a high priest after the order of Melchizedek.

Up to this point, the Lord Jesus has been shown to be superior to the prophets, the angels, and Moses. We now turn to the important theme of priesthood to see that Christ's high priesthood is of a superior order to Aaron's.

When God gave the law to Moses at Mount Sinai, He instituted a human priesthood by which the people might draw near to Himself. He decreed that the priests must be descended from the tribe of Levi and from the family of Aaron. This order is known as the Levitical or Aaronic priesthood.

Another divinely ordained priesthood is mentioned in the Old Testament, that of the patriarch Melchizedek. This man lived in the days of Abraham, long before the law was given, and served both as a king and a priest. In the passage before us the author will show that the Lord Jesus Christ is a priest after the order of Melchizedek, and that this order is superior to the Aaronic priesthood.

In the first four verses we have a description of the Aaronic priest. Then in verses 5-10 Christ's fitness as a priest is detailed.

5:1. The first qualification of the Aaronic priest was that he had to be chosen from among men. In other words, he had to be a man himself.

He was appointed to act on behalf of men in relation to God. He belonged to a special caste of men who served as intermediaries between men and God. One of his principal functions was to offer gifts and sacrifices for sins. Gifts refer to any offerings that were presented to God. Sacrifices refer to those special offerings in which blood was shed as atonement for sins.

5:2. He had to be able to sympathize with human frailty and to deal gently with the ignorant and wayward. His own frail flesh equipped him to understand the problems his people were facing.

The reference in this verse to the ignorant and the wayward is a reminder that the sacrifices in the Old Testament were for sins not done willfully. No provision was made for deliberate sin.

5:3. But while his being human was an advantage in that it identified him with the people, his sinful humanity was a disadvantage. He had to offer sacrifice for his own sins as well as for the sins of the people.

5:4. The office of priest was not something that men chose as a vocation. They had to be called to the work by God, just as Aaron was. God's call was limited to Aaron and to his descendants. No one outside that family could serve in the Tabernacle or the Temple.

5:5. The writer now turns to the Lord Jesus and demonstrates His fitness as a priest because of His divine appointment, His manifest humanity, and His acquired qualification.

As to His appointment, its source was God Himself. It was a sovereign call, having nothing to do with human genealogy. It involved a better relationship than any earthly priest ever had. Our priest is the unique Son of God, eternally begotten, begotten in incarnation, and begotten in resurrection.

5:6. Then Christ's priesthood is of a better order, for in Psalm 110:4 God declared Him to be a priest forever after the order of Melchizedek. This superiority will be explained more fully in chapter 7. The prominent thought here is that, unlike the Aaronic priesthood, this one is everlasting.

5:7. Christ is not only the sinless Son of God; He is also true Man. The writer refers to the variety of human experiences through which He passed "in the days of His flesh" to prove this. Notice the words used to describe His life and especially His experience in the garden of Gethsemane: prayers, supplications, loud cries, tears, sufferings. They all speak of His career as a dependent Man, living in obedience to God, and sharing all man's emotions that are not connected with sin.

Christ's prayer was not that He might be saved from dying; after all, His purpose in coming to the world was to die for sinners (John 12:27). His prayer was that He might be delivered *out of* death (JND), that His soul might not be left in Hades. This prayer was answered when God raised Him from the dead. He was heard because of His piety and devotion.

5:8. Now once again we come face to face with that profound mystery of the incarnation — how God could become Man in order to die for men.

Though He was a Son, or, better, Son though He was — He was not *a* Son, that is, one of many, but He was the only begotten Son of God. In spite of this tremendous fact, He learned obedience through what He suffered. His entrance into this world as a Man involved Him in experiences which He would never have known had He remained in Heaven. Each morning His ear was open to receive instructions from His Father for that day (Isaiah 50:4). He learned obedience experimentally as the Son who was always subject to His Father's will.

5:9. "And being made perfect. . . ." This cannot refer to His personal character because the Lord Jesus was always perfect. His words, His works, and His ways were absolutely flawless. In what sense then was He made perfect? The answer is in His office as our Saviour. He could never have become our perfect Saviour if He had remained in Heaven. But through His incarnation, death, burial, resurrection, and ascension, He completed the work that was necessary to save us from our sins, and now He has the acquired glory of being the perfect Saviour of the world.

Having returned to Heaven, He became the Author of eternal salvation to all who obey Him. He is the Source of salvation for all men, but only those who obey Him are saved.

Here salvation is conditional on obeying Him. In many other passages salvation is conditional on faith. How do we reconcile this seeming contradiction? First of all, it is the obedience of faith (Romans 1:5; 16:25-27): "the obedience which God requires is faith in His Word." But it is also true that saving faith is the kind that results in obedience. It is impossible to believe, in the true New Testament sense, without obeying.

5:10. Having gloriously accomplished the fundamental work of priesthood, the Lord Jesus was addressed by God as a High Priest after the order of Melchizedek.

It should be mentioned here that though Christ's priesthood is of the Melchizedekan order, yet His priestly functions are similar to those carried on by the Aaronic priests. In fact, the ministry of the Jewish priests was a foreshadow or picture of the work that Christ would accomplish.

IV. *Christ's High Priesthood Superior to Aaron's* (4:14—7:28) *(continued)*
  D. *Third Warning — the danger of falling away* (5:11—6:20)
    1. *Roadblock to learning* (5:11-14)
      a. *Deep truths and dull ears:* About this we have much to say which is hard to explain, since you have become dull of hearing.
      b. *Teachers and pupils:* For though by this time you ought to be teachers, you need some one to teach you again the first principles of God's word.
      c. *Solid food and milk:* You need milk, not solid food;
        (1) *Unskilled children:* for every one who lives on milk is unskilled in the word of righteousness, for he is a child.
        (2) *Discerning adults:* But solid food is for the mature, for those who have their faculties trained by practice to distinguish good from evil.

5:11. At this point the author must digress. He would like to continue with the subject of Christ's priesthood but he cannot. He is under divine constraint to rebuke his readers for their immaturity and at the same time to warn them seriously against the danger of falling away.

It is sadly true that our apprehension of divine truth is limited by our own spiritual condition. Dull ears cannot receive deep truths. How often it is true of us, as of the disciples, that the Lord has many things to say to us but we cannot bear them (John 16:12).

5:12. The writer reminds the Hebrews that they had been receiving instruction long enough now so that they should be teaching others. But the tragedy was that they still needed someone to teach them the ABC's of the Word of God.

"You ought to be teachers." God's order is that every believer should mature to the point where he can teach others. Each one teach one! While it is true that certain ones have a special gift of teaching, it is also true that every believer should engage in a teaching ministry. It was never God's intention that this work should be limited to a few.

"You need milk, not solid food." In the physical realm, a child who never advances from milk to solids is impaired. There is a form of stunted growth in the spiritual realm as well (1 Corinthians 3:2).

5:13. Professing believers who stay on a milk diet are inexperienced in the word of righteousness. They are hearers of the Word but not doers. They lose what they do not use, and remain in a state of perpetual infancy.

They do not have a keen sense of discernment in spiritual matters and are "tossed to and fro and carried about with every wind of doctrine, by the cunning of men, by their craftiness in deceitful wiles" (Ephesians 4:14).

5:14. Solid spiritual food is for full-grown men, for those who have exercised their spiritual senses to discern good and evil. By obeying the light they receive from God's Word, these men are able to form spiritual judgments and to save themselves from moral and doctrinal dangers.

In this context the particular sense in which the readers are urged to distinguish between good and evil is in relation to Christianity and Judaism. Not that Judaism was evil in itself; the Levitical system was introduced by God Himself. But it was intended to point forward to Christ. He is the fulfillment of the ceremonial types and shadows. Now that Christ has come, it is sinful to return to the pictures of Him. Anything that rivals Christ in the affections and loyalties of men is evil. Spiritually mature believers are able to discern between the inferiority of the Aaronic priesthood and the superiority of Christ's.

CHAPTER 6

IV. *Christ's High Priesthood Superior to Aaron's* (4:14—7:28) *(continued)*

    D. *Third warning — the danger of falling away* (5:11—6:20) *(continued)*

        2. *Progressing to maturity* (6:1-3)

            a. *Fundamental Old Testament doctrines:* Therefore let us leave the elementary doctrines of Christ

            b. *Full growth:* and go on to maturity,

            c. *Foundation truths:* not laying again a foundation

                (1) *Repentance:* of repentance from dead works

                (2) *Faith:* and of faith toward God,

                (3) *Washings:* with instruction about ablutions,

                (4) *Laying on of hands:* the laying on of hands,

                (5) *Resurrection:* the resurrection of the dead,

                (6) *Judgment:* and eternal judgment,

            d. *Fixed purpose:* And this we will do if God permits.

        3. *Relapsing into apostasy* (6:4-8)

            a. *The clear impossibility:* For it is impossible to restore again to repentance

b. *The class involved:* those who have once been enlightened, who have tasted the heavenly gift, and have become partakers of the Holy Spirit, and have tasted the goodness of the word of God and the powers of the age to come,

c. *The cardinal sin:* if they then commit apostasy,

d. *The condemning implications:*
   (1) *Crucifying God's Son:* since they crucify the Son of God on their own account
   (2) *Consigning Him to contempt:* and hold Him up to contempt.

e. *The counterpart in nature*
   (1) *Conditions of blessing:* For land which has drunk the rain that often falls upon it, and brings forth vegetation useful to those for whose sake it is cultivated, receives a blessing from God.
   (2) *Conditions of cursing:* But if it bears thorns and thistles, it is worthless and near to being cursed; its end is to be burned.

6:1. The warning which began in 5:11 continues throughout this chapter. It is one of the most controversial and disturbing passages in the entire New Testament. Since so many godly Christians are disagreed on its interpretation, we must not speak with dogmatism. All we can do is to present the explanation which appeals to us as being most consistent with the context and with the rest of the New Testament.

First of all, the readers are exhorted to leave the elementary doctrines of Christ, literally, "the word of the beginning of Christ" (F.W. Grant), or "the beginning word of the Christ" (Wuest). We understand this to mean the basic doctrines of religion that were taught in the Old Testament and that were designed to prepare the people of Israel for the coming of the Messiah. These doctrines are listed in the latter part of verse 1 and in verse 2. As we shall seek to show, they are not the fundamental doctrines of Christianity but rather teachings of an elementary nature which formed the foundation for later building. The exhortation is to leave these basics, not in the sense of abandoning them as worthless, but rather of advancing from them to maturity. The implication is that the period of Judaism was a time of spiritual infancy. Christianity represents full growth.

Once a foundation has been laid, the next step is to build upon it. A doctrinal foundation was laid in the Old Testament; it included the six fundamental teachings which are now listed. These represent a starting point. The great New Testament truths concerning Christ, His Person, and His work, represent the ministry of maturity.

The first Old Testament doctrine is repentance from dead works. This was preached constantly by the prophets as well as by the forerunner of the Messiah. They all called upon people to turn from works that were dead in the sense that they were devoid of faith.

Dead works here may also refer to works which formerly were right, but which now are dead since Christ has come. For example, all the services connected with temple worship are outmoded by the finished work of Christ.

Secondly, the writer mentions faith in God. This again is an Old Testament emphasis. In the New Testament Christ is almost invariably presented as the object of faith. Not that this displaces faith in God; but a faith in God which leaves out Christ is now inadequate.

6:2. Instruction about ablutions refers not to Christian baptism, as one might conclude from the AV, but to the ceremonial washings which figured so prominently in the religious lives of the priests and people of Israel (see also 9:10).

The ritual of laying on of hands is described in Leviticus 1:4; 3:2; 16:21. The offerer or the priest laid his hands on the head of an animal as an act of identification. In figure, the animal bore away the sins of the people who were associated with it. This ceremony typified vicarious atonement. We do not believe that there is any reference here to the laying on of hands as practiced by the apostles and others in the early church (Acts 8:17; 13:3; 19:6).

The resurrection of the dead is taught in Job 19:25-27 (AV); Psalm 17:15; and it is implied in Isaiah 53:10-12. What was seen only indistinctly in the Old

Testament is brightly revealed in the New (2 Timothy 1:10).

The final foundational truth of the Old Testament was eternal judgment (Psalm 9:17; Isaiah 66:24).

These first principles represented Judaism, and were preparatory to the coming of Christ. Christians should not continue to be content with these but should press on to the fuller revelation they now have in Christ. The readers are urged to pass "from shadow to substance, from type to antitype, from husk to kernel, from the dead forms of the religion of their ancestors to the living realities in Christ."

6:3. The author expresses his desire to help them do this, if God permits. However, the limiting factor will be on their side and not on God's. God will enable them to advance to full spiritual manhood, but they must respond to the Word positively by exercising true faith and endurance.

6:4. We come now to the heart of the warning against apostasy. It applies to a class of people whom it is impossible to restore again to repentance. Apparently these people had once repented (though no mention is made of their faith in Christ). Now it is clearly stated that a renewed repentance is impossible.

Who are these people? The answer is given in verses 4 and 5. In examining the great privileges which they enjoyed, it should be noticed that all these things could be true of the unsaved. It is never clearly stated that they had been born again. Neither is any mention made of such essentials as saving faith, redemption by His blood, or eternal life.

They had once been enlightened. They had heard the gospel of the grace of God. They were not in darkness concerning the way of salvation. Judas Iscariot had been enlightened but he rejected the light.

They tasted the heavenly gift. The Lord Jesus is the heavenly Gift. They had tasted of Him but had never received Him by a definite act of faith. It is possible to taste without eating or drinking. When men offered wine mixed with gall to Jesus on the cross, He tasted it but He would not drink it (Matthew 27:34). It is not enough to taste Christ; unless we eat the flesh of the Son of man and drink His blood, that is, unless we truly receive Him as Lord and Saviour, we have no life in us (John 6:53).

They had become partakers of the Holy Spirit. Before we jump to the conclusion that this necessarily implies conversion, we should remember that the Holy Spirit carries on a preconversion ministry in men's lives. He sanctifies unbelievers (1 Corinthians 7:14), putting them in a position of external privilege. He convicts unbelievers of sin, of righteousness, and of judgment (John 16:8). He leads men to repentance and points them to Christ as their only hope. Men may thus partake of the Holy Spirit without being indwelt by Him.

6:5. They had "tasted the goodness of the word of God." As they heard the gospel preached, they were strangely moved and drawn to it. They were like the seed that fell on rocky ground; they heard the Word and immediately received it with joy, but they had no root in themselves. They endured for a while, but when tribulation or persecution arose on account of the Word, they promptly fell away (Matthew 13:20-21).

They had tasted "the powers of the age to come." "Powers" here means "miracles." "The age to come" is the millennial age, the coming era of peace and prosperity when Christ will reign over the earth for a thousand years. The miracles which accompanied the preaching of the gospel in the early days of the Church (Hebrews 2:4) were a foretaste of signs and wonders which will be performed in Christ's kingdom. These people had witnessed these miracles in the first century, in fact, they might have participated in them. Take, for instance, the miracle of the loaves and fishes. After Jesus had fed the five thousand, the people followed Him to the other side of the sea. The Saviour realized that, though they had tasted a miracle, they did not really believe in Him. He said to them, "Truly, truly, I say to you, you seek Me, not because you saw signs, but because you ate your fill of the loaves" (John 6:26).

6:6. If a man falls away, after enjoying the privileges just enumerated, it is impossible to renew him to repentance. He has committed the sin of apostasy. He has reached the place where the lights go out on the way to hell.

Apostates are people who hear the gospel, who make a profession of being Christians, who become identified with a Christian assembly, and who then abandon their profession of faith, decisively repudiate Christ, desert the Christian fellowship, and take their place with enemies of the Lord Jesus Christ. Apostasy is a sin which can be committed only by unbelievers, not by those who are deceived but by those who knowingly, willfully, and maliciously turn against the Lord.

It should not be confused with the sin of the average unbeliever who hears the gospel but does nothing about it. For instance, a man may fail to respond to Christ after repeated invitations from the Holy Spirit. But he is not an apostate. He can still be saved if he will commit himself to the Saviour. Of course, if he dies in unbelief, he is lost forever, but he is not hopeless as long as he is capable of exercising faith in the Lord.

Apostasy should not be confused with backsliding. A true believer may wander very far away from Christ. Through sin his fellowship with God is shattered. He may even reach the point where he is no longer recognized as a Christian. But he can be restored to full fellowship as soon as he confesses and forsakes his sin (1 John 1:9).

Apostasy is not the same as the unpardonable sin mentioned in the Gospels. That was the sin of attributing the miracles of the Lord Jesus to the prince of the demons. His miracles were actually performed in the power of the Holy Spirit. To attribute them to the devil was tantamount to blaspheming the Holy Spirit. It implied that the Holy Spirit was the devil. Jesus said that such a sin could never be forgiven, either in that age or in the age to come (Mark 3:22-30). Apostasy is similar to blasphemy against the Holy Spirit in that it is an eternal sin, but there the resemblance ends.

We believe that apostasy is the same as the sin unto death mentioned in 1 John 5:16b (AV). John was writing about people who had professed to be believers and had participated in the activities of local churches. Then they had imbibed the false teaching of the gnostics and had spitefully left the Christian fellowship. Their deliberate departure indicated that they had never been truly born again (1 John 2:19). By openly denying that Jesus is the Christ (1 John 2:22), they had committed the sin unto death, and it was useless to pray for their recovery (1 John 5:16b).

Oftentimes earnest Christians are troubled when they read Hebrews 6 and similar passages. Satan uses these verses especially to unsettle believers who are having physical, mental, or emotional difficulties. They fear that they have fallen away from Christ and that there is no hope for their restoration. They worry that they have drifted beyond redemption's point. The fact that they are even concerned about it is conclusive evidence that they are not apostates. An apostate would not have any such fears; he would brazenly repudiate Christ.

If the sin of apostasy does not apply to believers, to whom then does it apply in our day? It applies, for instance, to a young man who makes a profession of faith in Christ and seems to go on brightly for a while, but then something happens in his life. Perhaps he experiences bitter persecution. Perhaps he falls into gross immorality. Or perhaps he goes off to college and is shaken by the anti-Christian arguments of atheistic teachers. With full knowledge of the truth, he deliberately turns away from it. He completely renounces Christ and viciously tramples on every sacred, fundamental doctrine of the Christian faith. The Bible says it is impossible to restore such an one to repent-ance, and experience corroborates the Bible. We have known many who have apostasized from Christ, but we have never known one who has returned to Him.

As we approach the end of this age, we can expect a rising tide of apostasy (2 Thessalonians 2:3 AV; 1 Timothy 4:1). Therefore the warning against falling away becomes more relevant with every day that passes.

The enormous guilt of apostates is indicated in the words: "since they crucify the Son of God on their own account and hold Him up to contempt" (verse 6b). This signifies a deliberate, malicious spurning of Christ, not just a careless disregard of Him. It indicates a positive betrayal of Him, a joining of forces against Him, and a ridiculing of His Person and work.

6:7. Now the writer turns to the world of nature to find a counterpart to the true believer (verse 7) and to the apostate (verse 8). In both cases the person is likened to the land. The privileges listed in verses 4 and 5 are compared to the invigorating rain. The crop of vegetation speaks of the ultimate response of the person to the privileges received. This in turn determines whether the land is blessed or cursed.

The true believer is like the land that receives the rain, brings forth useful vegetation, and is blessed by God.

6:8. The apostate is like land that also is well watered but it brings forth nothing but thorns and thistles, the fruit of sin. It receives but never produces useful plants. Such land is worthless. It is condemned already. Its destiny is to be burned.

IV. *Christ's High Priesthood Superior to Aaron's* (4:14—7:28) *(continued)*

　D. *Third warning — the danger of falling away* (5:11—6:20) *(continued)*

　　4. *Evidencing reality* (6:9-12)

　　　a. *Confidence concerning God's loved ones:* Though we speak thus, yet in your case, beloved, we feel sure of better things that belong to salvation.

　　　b. *Reason for this confidence:* For God is not so unjust as to overlook your work and the love which you showed for His sake in serving the saints, as you still do.

　　　c. *Desire for all others*

　　　　(1) *Full assurance of salvation:* And we desire each one of you to show the same earnestness in realizing the full assurance of hope until the end,

　　　　(2) *True followers of the faithful:* so that you may not be sluggish, but imitators of those who through faith and patience inherit the promises.

6:9. There are two strong indications in verses 9 and 10 that the apostates described in the preceding verses are unbelievers. First, there is the abrupt change in pronouns. In discussing apostates, the writer refers to them as "they." Now in addressing true believers, he uses the pronouns "you" and "your."

The second indication is even clearer. Speaking to

believers, he says, "Though we speak thus, yet in your case, beloved, we feel sure of better things that belong to salvation." The inference is that the things he had described in verses 4-6 and 8 do not accompany salvation.

6:10. Two of the things that accompany salvation were manifest in the lives of the saints — their work and their love. Their faith manifested itself in a life of good works, and they had the hallmark of true Christianity — love for the household of faith. They continued to serve the Lord's people for His sake.

6:11. The next two verses seem to be written to a different class of people; namely, to those of whom the writer was not sure. These were the ones who seemed to be in danger of drifting back into Judaism.

First, he expresses the desire that they will show the same earnestness as the true believers have shown in realizing the full assurance of hope until the end. He wants them to go on steadfastly for Christ until the final hope of the Christian is realized in Heaven. This is a proof of reality.

6:12. They should not be sluggish, allowing their feet to drag and their spirits to lag. They should press on, imitating all true believers who through faith and long-suffering inherit the promises.

IV. *Christ's   High   Priesthood   Superior   to   Aaron's* (4:14—7:28) *(continued)*
    D. *Third warning — the danger of falling away* (5:11—6:20) *(continued)*
       5. *Exhibiting faith and patience* (6:13-20)

a. *The example of Abraham*
- (1) *The divine promise:* For when God made a promise to Abraham,
- (2) *The divine dilemma:* since He had no one greater by whom to swear,
- (3) *The divine oath:* He swore by Himself,
- (4) *The divine promise:* saying, "Surely I will bless you and multiply you."
- (5) *The divine fulfillment:* And thus Abraham, having patiently endured, obtained the promise.

b. *The basis of human credence:*
- (1) *Swear by a greater:* Men indeed swear by a greater than themselves,
- (2) *Settle all disputes:* and in all their disputes an oath is final for confirmation.

c. *The basis of divine credence*
- (1) *God's desire:* So when God desired to show more convincingly to the heirs of the promise the unchangeable character of His purpose,
- (2) *God's oath:* He interposed with an oath,
- (3) *Faith's dual foundation:* so that through two unchangeable things,
- (4) *Faith's sure conviction:* in which it is impossible that God should prove false,
- (5) *Faith's pilgrim migration:* we who have fled for refuge

        (6) *Faith's strong motivation:* might have strong encouragement to seize the hope set before us.

   d. *Our unmovable hope*

       (1) *Our soul's anchor:* We have this as a sure and steadfast anchor of the soul,

       (2) *Its sure location:* a hope that enters into the inner shrine behind the curtain,

       (3) *Our glorious Forerunner:* where Jesus has gone as a forerunner on our behalf,

       (4) *His eternal priesthood:* having become a high priest for ever after the order of Melchizedek.

6:13. This closing section of the chapter is linked with the exhortation in verse 12 to press on with confidence and patience. The example of Abraham is given as a stimulus and the certainty of the believer's hope is affirmed.

In one sense, the Christian may seem to be at a disadvantage. He has given up all for Christ, and has nothing material to show for it. Everything is in the future. How then can he be sure that his hope is not in vain?

The answer is found in God's promise to Abraham, a promise that included in germ form all that He would later bestow in the Person of Christ. When God made that promise, He swore by Himself since He could not swear by anyone greater.

6:14. The promise is found in Genesis 22:16-17: "By Myself I have sworn, says the Lord . . . I will indeed bless you, and I will multiply your descendants. . . ." God pledged Himself to carry out this promise, and therefore its fulfillment was assured.

6:15. Abraham believed God; he patiently endured; and he received the fulfillment. Actually Abraham was not taking a chance in believing God. No risk was involved. The Word of God is the surest thing in the universe. Any promise of God is as certain of fulfillment as if it had already taken place.

6:16. In human affairs, men swear by someone greater than themselves. In courts of law, for example, they promise to tell the truth and then add, "so help me, God." They appeal to God for confirmation that what they are going to say is true.

When men take an oath to confirm a promise, that normally ends all debate. It is understood that the promise will be kept.

6:17. God wanted His believing people to be absolutely assured that what He promised would come to pass. Actually His bare promise would have been enough, but He wanted to demonstrate it to a greater extent than even by a promise. So He added an oath to the promise.

"The heirs of the promise" are all those who by faith are children of faithful Abraham. The promise referred to is the promise of eternal salvation to all who believe on Him. When God made the promise of a seed to Abraham, the promise found its full and ultimate fulfillment in Christ, and all the blessings that flow from union with Christ were therefore included in the promise.

6:18. The believer now has two unchangeable things on which to rely — His Word and His oath. It is impossible to imagine anything more secure or certain. God promises to save all who believe on Christ; then He confirms it with an oath. The conclusion is inevitable: the believer is eternally secure.

In the remainder of the chapter the writer employs four figures to drive home the utter reliability of the Christian hope:

> a city of refuge
> an anchor
> a Forerunner
> a High Priest

First, those who are true believers are pictured as fleeing from this doomed world to the heavenly city of refuge. To encourage them in their flight, God has given them an unfailing hope based upon His Word and His oath.

6:19. In the storms and trials of life this hope serves as an anchor of the soul. The knowledge that our glorification is as certain as if it had already happened keeps us from drifting on the wild waves of doubt and despair.

The anchor is not cast in the shifting sands of this world but takes hold in the heavenly sanctuary. Since our hope is the anchor, the meaning is that our hope is secured in the very presence of God. Just as sure as the anchor is there, we shall be there also.

6:20. The Lord Jesus has gone into the inner shrine

also as our Forerunner. His presence there insures the ultimate entrance of all who belong to Him. It is no exaggeration to say that the simplest believer on earth is as certain of Heaven as the saints who are already there.

The fourth figure is that of High Priest. Our Lord has become a High Priest forever after the order of Melchizedek. His eternal priesthood guarantees our eternal preservation. Just as surely as we have been reconciled to God by His death, so surely are we saved by His life as our Priest at God's right hand (Romans 5:10).

This mention of Christ as High Priest after the order of Melchizedek reminds us that this subject was interrupted at 5:10 when the author digressed on the extended warning against apostasy. Now he is ready to resume his theme that Christ's high priesthood is superior to Aaron's. He has skillfully returned to the main flow of argument.

CHAPTER 7

IV. *Christ's High Priesthood Superior to Aaron's* (4:14–7:28) *(continued)*
   E. *Historical facts concerning Melchizedek* (7:1-3)
      1. *His offices:* For this Melchizedek, king of Salem, priest of the most high God,
      2. *His relation to Abraham*
         a. *Blesser:* met Abraham returning from the slaughter of the kings and blessed him;
         b. *Receiver of tithes:* and to him Abraham apportioned a tenth part of everything.
      3. *His personal character:* He is first, by translation of his name, king of righteousness, and then he is also king of Salem, that is, king of peace.
      4. *His recorded genealogy:* He is without father or mother or genealogy,
      5. *His recorded vital statistics:* and has neither beginning of days nor end of life,
      6. *His perpetual priesthood:* but resembling the Son of God he continues a priest for ever.

7:1. Melchizedek was an enigmatical figure who appeared briefly on the stage of human history, then disappeared. Centuries later his name was mentioned by the Psalmist David. Then, after a lapse of additional centuries, it reappears in the book of Hebrews. One thing is apparent: God arranged the details of his life so that he would be an excellent type of our Lord Jesus Christ.

In these first three verses of chapter 7 we have some historical facts concerning him. We are reminded that he combined the offices of king and priest in his person. He was king of Salem (later called Jerusalem), and priest of the most high God. He was the political and spiritual leader of his people. This is, of course, God's ideal — that there should be no separation between the secular and the sacred. When sinful man is reigning it is necessary to separate church and state. Only when Christ reigns in righteousness will it be possible to unite the two (Isaiah 32:1,17).

Melchizedek met Abraham when the latter was returning from a military victory and blessed him. The significance of this act is reserved for verse 7. If we had only the Old Testament Scriptures, we would never realize the deep significance of these seemingly irrelevant details.

7:2. Abraham took a tenth part of the spoils of war and gave it to this mysterious king-priest. Again we must wait till verses 4,6,8-10 to learn the hidden meaning of Abraham's tithe.

In the Scriptures, a man's name stands for what he is. We learn about Melchizedek's personal character from his name and his title: his name means king of righteousness and his title (king of Salem) means king of peace.

It is not without meaning that righteousness is mentioned first, then peace. There cannot be peace unless first there is righteousness.

We see this clearly in the work of Christ. At the cross, "mercy and truth . . . met together; righteousness and peace . . . kissed each other" (Psalm 85:10 AV). Because the Saviour met all the righteous demands of God against our sins, we can have peace with God.

7:3. The puzzle concerning Melchizedek deepens when we read that he had neither father, mother, genealogy, birth, nor death. If we divorce these statements from their context, we would have to conclude that he was a visitor from Heaven or from another planet, or that he was a special creation of God.

But the key to understanding lies in taking these statements in their context. The subject is priesthood. The writer is distinguishing between the Melchizedekan priesthood and the Aaronic. In order to qualify for the Aaronic priesthood a man had to be born of the tribe of Levi and of the family of Aaron. Genealogy was all-important. Also, his qualification began at birth and ended at death.

Melchizedek's priesthood was quite different. He did not inherit the priesthood by being born into a priestly family. God simply picked him out and designated him as a priest. *As far as his priesthood was concerned,* there is no record of his father, mother, or genealogy. In his case, this was not of importance, *and as far as the record is concerned,* no mention is made of his birth or death; therefore his priesthood continues.

We should not conclude that Melchizedek had no parents, that he was never born, and that he never died. That is not the point. The thought is that as far as his priesthood was concerned, there is no record of these vital statistics because his ministry as priest was not dependent on them.

He was not the Son of God, as some have mistakenly thought, but resembled the Son of God in this respect, that his priesthood continued without interruption.

IV. *Christ's   High   Priesthood   Superior   to   Aaron's* (4:14–7:28) *(continued)*

    F. *Melchizedek's priesthood superior to Aaron's* (7:4-25)

        1. *The argument concerning tithes* (7:4-10)

            a. *Abraham paid tithes to Melchizedek:* See how great he is! Abraham the patriarch gave him a tithe of the spoils.

                (1) *The usual Aaronic order:* And those descendants of Levi who receive the priestly office have a commandment in the law to take tithes from the people, that is, from their brethren, though these also are descended from Abraham.

                (2) *The unusual Melchizedekan order:* But this man who has not their genealogy received tithes from Abraham

            b. *Melchizedek blessed Abraham*

                (1) *The fact stated:* and blessed him who

had the promises.

    (2) *The conclusion drawn:* It is beyond dispute that the inferior is blessed by the superior.

  c. *The duration of the two priesthoods*

    (1) *The mortal Aaronic priesthood:* Here tithes are received by mortal men;

    (2) *The enduring Melchizedekan priesthood:* there, by one of whom it is testified that he lives.

  d. *Levi paid tithes to Melchizedek*

    (1) *The suggestion:* One might even say that Levi himself, who receives tithes, paid tithes through Abraham,

    (2) *The explanation:* for he was still in the loins of his ancestor when Melchizedek met him.

Now the author is going to demonstrate that Melchizedek's priesthood is superior to Aaron's. There are three arguments in the proof: the argument concerning tithes and blessing; the argument concerning a change that has taken place, replacing the Aaronic priesthood; and the argument concerning perpetuity of the Melchizedekan priesthood.

7:4. In verses 4-10 we have the first argument. It opens with an unusual interjection, asking the readers to consider the greatness of Melchizedek. Abraham gave him a tenth part of the spoils of battle. Since Abraham was one of the greatest stars in the Hebrew firmament, it follows that Melchizedek must have been a star of even greater magnitude.

7:5. As far as the Levitical priests were concerned, they were authorized by the law to collect tithes from their fellow Hebrews. Both the priests and the people traced their descent from Abraham.

7:6. But when Abraham paid tithes to Melchizedek, it was an unusual and unconventional transaction. Abraham, called to be the father of the nation from which Messiah would come, was paying deference to one who was not connected with the chosen people. Melchizedek's priesthood leaped over racial barriers.

Another significant fact is that Melchizedek blessed Abraham. He said, "Blessed be Abram by God Most High, maker of heaven and earth" (Genesis 14:19-20).

7:7. When one man blesses another man, it is understood that the superior blesses the inferior. This does not signify any personal or moral inferiority, of course, but simply an inferiority of position.

As we read these arguments based on the Old Testament Scriptures, we should try to picture the reactions of the Hebrew readers. They had always revered Abraham as one of their greatest national heroes, and rightly so. But now they learn that Abraham acknowledged a "non-Jewish" priest as his superior. Just think that this was in their Bible all the time and they had never noticed it!

7:8. In the Aaronic priesthood tithes were received by men who were subject to death. There was a constant succession of priests, each one serving his own generation, then passing on. In Melchizedek's case there is no mention of his having died. Therefore he represents a priesthood which is unique in that it is perpetual.

7:9. In receiving tithes from Abraham, Melchizedek virtually received them from Levi. Since Levi was the head of the priestly tribe, it amounts to saying that the Aaronic priesthood paid tithes to Melchizedek and this acknowledged the superiority of the latter.

7:10. By what chain of reasoning can it be said that Levi paid tithes to Melchizedek? Well, first of all, Abraham was actually the one who paid the tithes. He was the great-grandfather of Levi. Though Levi had not yet been born, he was in the loins of Abraham, that is, he was destined to be descended from the patriarch. Abraham really acted as a representative for all his posterity when he gave a tenth to Melchizedek. Therefore Levi, and the priesthood that sprang from him, took second place to Melchizedek and to his priesthood.

IV. *Christs High Priesthood Superior to Aaron's* (4:14—7:28) *(continued)*

   F. *Melchizedek's priesthood superior to Aaron's* (7:4-25) *(continued)*

      2. *The argument concerning change in priesthood* (7:11-22)

         a. *A change in the order of priesthood:*

            (1) *Levitical priesthood imperfect:* Now if perfection had been attainable through the Levitical priesthood (for under it the people received the law),

      (2) *New priest necessary:* what further need would there have been for another priest to arise after the order of Melchizedek, rather than one named after the order of Aaron?

  b. *A change in the law of priesthood:* For when there is a change in the priesthood, there is necessarily a change in the law as well.

      (1) *General explanation:* For the one of whom these things are spoken belonged to another tribe, from which no one has ever served at the altar.

      (2) *Specific designation:* For it is evident that our Lord was descended from Judah, and in connection with that tribe Moses said nothing about priests.

      (3) *Added authentication:* This becomes even more evident when another priest arises in the likeness of Melchizedek,

        (a) *Not by carnal commandment:* who has become a priest, not according to a legal requirement concerning bodily descent

        (b) *But by inherent power:* but by the power of an indestructible life.

      (4) *Scriptural authorization:* For it is

witnessed of Him, "Thou art a priest for ever, after the order of Melchizedek."

(5) *Distinct abrogation:* On the one hand, a former commandment is set aside because of its weakness and uselessness (for the law made nothing perfect);

(6) *Superior innovation:* on the other hand, a better hope is introduced, through which we draw near to God.

c. *A change in the mode of induction:* And it was not without an oath.

(1) *The old order:* Those who formerly became priests took their office without an oath,

(2) *The new order:* but this one was addressed with an oath,

(3) *The form of the oath:* "The Lord has sworn and will not change His mind, 'Thou art a priest for ever.'"

(4) *The covenant's Surety:* This makes Jesus the surety of a better covenant.

7:11. In verses 11-22 we find the second argument that shows Melchizedek's priesthood to be superior to Aaron's. The argument is that there has been a change in the priesthood. The priesthood of Christ has set aside the Levitical priesthood. This would not have been necessary if the latter had achieved its purpose fully and finally.

The fact is that perfection was not attainable through the Levitical system. Sins were never put away and the worshipers never obtained rest of conscience. The priesthood that was set up under the law of Moses was not the ultimate one.

Another kind of priesthood is now in effect. The perfect Priest has now come, and His priesthood is not reckoned after the order of Aaron but rather after the order of Melchizedek.

7:12. The fact that the order of priesthood has been changed forces the conclusion that the entire legal structure on which the priesthood was based has been changed also. This is a very radical announcement. Like a tolling bell, it rings out the old order of things and rings in the new.

7:13. That there has been a change in the law is evident from the fact that the Lord Jesus belonged to a tribe which was barred from performing priestly functions by the Levitical law.

7:14. It was from the tribe of Judah that our great High Priest was descended. The Mosaic legislation never authorized anyone from that tribe to be a priest. Yet Jesus is a Priest. How can that be? Because the law has been changed.

7:15. The author has additional evidence that there has been a vast change in the law of priesthood. Another kind of Priest has arisen in the likeness of Melchizedek, and His qualification for the office is quite different from that of Aaron's sons.

7:16. The Levitical priests became eligible by meeting the legal requirements concerning bodily descent.

They had to be born of the tribe of Levi and of the family of Aaron.

But what qualifies the Lord to be a Priest like Melchizedek is His indestructible life. It is not a question of pedigree but of personal, inherent power. He lives forever.

7:17. This is confirmed by the words of Psalm 110:4, where David points forward to the Messiah's priesthood: "You are a priest for ever after the order of Melchizedek." Here the emphasis is on the word "for ever." His ministry will never cease because His life will never end.

7:18. The law which set up the Aaronic priesthood has been disannulled because it was weak and unprofitable. It has been disannulled by the advent of Christ.

In what sense was the law weak and unprofitable? Was it not given by God Himself? Could God give anything that was impotent and useless? The answer is that God never intended this to be the ultimate law of priesthood. It was preparatory to the coming of God's ideal priesthood. It was a partial and temporary picture of that which would be perfect and final.

7:19. It was also weak and useless in the sense that it made nothing perfect. The people were never able to go into the presence of God in the most holy place. This enforced distance between God and man was a constant reminder that the sin question was not settled once for all.

But now a better hope has been introduced by which we draw near to God. That better hope is the Lord Jesus Himself; those who have Him as their only hope have perfect access to God at any time.

7:20. Not only has there been a change in the order of priesthood and in the law of priesthood, but also, as we shall now see, there has been a change in the method of induction. The reasoning here revolves around the use of God's oath in connection with Christ's priesthood. The oath signifies the introduction of that which is unchangeable and everlasting. "Nothing less than the oath of Almighty God guarantees the efficacy and the eternity of the priesthood of our blessed Lord Jesus" (Rainsbury).

7:21. The Aaronic priests were not appointed with an oath. Therefore the implication is that their priesthood was intended to be provisional and not enduring.

But God addressed Christ with an oath in designating Him as a priest. The form of the oath is found in Psalm 110:4: "The Lord has sworn and will not change His mind, 'You are a priest for ever after the order of Melchizedek.' " "God places behind Christ's commission the eternal verities of His throne, and the immutable attributes of His nature. If they can change, the new priesthood can change. Otherwise it cannot" (Henderson).

7:22. It follows from this that Jesus is the Surety of a better covenant. The Aaronic priesthood was a part of the old covenant. The priesthood of Christ is connected with the new covenant. Covenant and priesthood stand or fall together.

The new covenant is an unconditional convenant of grace which God will make with the house of Israel and with the house of Judah when the Lord Jesus sets up His kingdom on the earth (Jeremiah 31:33-34). Believers today enjoy some of the blessings of the new covenant but its complete fulfillment will not be realized until Israel is restored and redeemed nationally.

Jesus is the Surety of the new covenant in the sense that He Himself is the Guarantee. By His death, burial, and resurrection, He provided a righteous basis upon which God can fulfill the terms of the covenant. His endless priesthood is also vitally linked with the unfailing fulfillment of the terms of the covenant.

IV. *Christ's Priesthood Superior to Aaron's* (4:14—7:28) (continued)

   F. *Melchizedek's priesthood superior to Aaron's* (7:4-25) *(continued)*

      3. *The argument concerning perpetuity* (7:23-25)

         a. *The former priests*

           (1) *Numerous:* The former priests were many in number,

           (2) *Noncontinuous:* because they were prevented by death from continuing in office;

         b. *The new Priest*

           (1) *Perpetual priesthood:* but He holds His priesthood permanently,

           (2) *Endless life:* because He continues for ever.

           (3) *Perfect salvation:* Consequently He is able for all time to save those who

        draw near to God through Him,

(4) *Constant   intercession:*   since   He
always lives to make intercession for
them.

7:23. We now come to the third and final argument concerning the superiority of the Melchizedekan priesthood.

The priests of Israel were numerous. It is said that there were eighty-four high priests in the history of the nation, and of course there were numberless lesser priests. The office periodically changed hands because of the death of the incumbents. The ministry suffered from these inevitable interruptions.

7:24. In the case of Christ's priesthood, there is no such failure because He lives forever. His priesthood is never passed on to anyone else, and there is no interruption to its effectiveness. It is unchangeable and intransmissible.

7:25. Because He lives forever He is able to save to the uttermost those who come to God by Him. We generally understand this to refer to His work in saving sinners from the penalty of sin, but actually the writer is here speaking of Christ's work in saving saints from the power of sin. It is not so much His role as Saviour as that of High Priest. There is no danger that any believers will be lost. Their eternal security rests upon His perpetual intercession for them. He is able to save them for all time because His present ministry for them at God's right hand can never be interrupted by death.

IV. *Christ's Priesthood Superior to Aaron's* (4:14—7:28) *(continued)*

   G. *Christ's priesthood superior to Aaron's because of His personal excellence* (7:26-28)

   1. *Spotless character:* For it was fitting that we should have such a high priest, holy, blameless, unstained, separated from sinners,

   2. *Highest exaltation:* exalted above the heavens.

   3. *Perfect sacrifice*

      a. *Unnecessary repetition:* He has no need, like those high priests, to offer sacrifices daily, first for His own sins and then for those of the people;

      b. *Final oblation:* He did this once for all

      c. *Marvelous condescension:* when He offered up Himself.

   4. *Superior appointment*

      a. *The law's high priests:* Indeed, the law appoints men in their weakness as high priests,

      b. *The oath's High Priest:* but the word of the oath, which came later than the law, appoints a Son who has been made perfect for ever.

7:26. Christ's priesthood is superior to Aaron's because of His personal excellence. He is holy in His standing before God. He is blameless or guileless in His dealings with men. He is unstained in His personal character. He is separated from sinners in His life at God's right hand. He is made higher than the heavens in His present and eternal splendor. It is fitting that we should have such a High Priest.

7:27. Unlike the Levitical priests, our High Priest does not need to offer sacrifices daily; He did this once for all. He does not need to offer for His own sins because He is absolutely sinless. A third amazing way in which He differs from the former priests is that He offered Himself for the sins of the people. The Priest gave Himself as the sacrifice. Wonderful grace of Jesus!

7:28. The law sets up priests who are personally imperfect; they are characterized by weakness and failure; they are only ritually holy.

God's oath, given after the law, appoints His Son as a Priest who is perfect forever. This oath was referred to in verse 21 of this chapter and quoted from Psalm 110:4.

There are momentous implications in the material we have just covered. Human priesthood has been superseded by a divine and eternal priesthood. How foolish, then, for men to set up priestly systems patterned after the Old Testament and to intrude upon the functions of our Great High Priest.

CHAPTER 8

V. *Christ's Ministry Superior to Aaron's* (8:1-13)
   A. *The two sanctuaries contrasted* (8:1-6)
      1. *The heavenly sanctuary*
         a. *The Priest:* Now the point in what we are saying is this: we have such a high priest,
            (1) *Posture:* one who is seated
            (2) *Place:* at the right hand of the throne of the Majesty in heaven,
         b. *His sanctuary*
            (1) *Its character:* a minister in the sanctuary and the true tent
            (2) *Its construction:* which is set up not by man but by the Lord.
         c. *His ministry*
            (1) *Usual responsibility:* For every high priest is appointed to offer gifts and sacrifices;
            (2) *Consequent necessity:* hence it is necessary for this priest also to have something to offer.
      2. *The earthly Tabernacle*
         a. *The priests*
            (1) *Legal ineligibility:* Now if He were on earth, He would not be a priest at all,

        (2) *Lawful incumbency:* since there are priests who offer gifts according to the law.

   b. *The sanctuary*

      (1) *A copy of the reality:* They serve a copy and shadow of the heavenly sanctuary;

      (2) *Scriptural proof:* for when Moses was about to erect the tent, he was instructed by God, saying, "See that you make everything according to the pattern which was shown you on the mountain."

  3. *Christ's more excellent ministry*

   a. *Better ministry:* But as it is, Christ has obtained a ministry which is as much more excellent than the old

   b. *Better covenant:* as the covenant He mediates is better,

   c. *Better promises:* since it is enacted on better promises.

8:1. In the verses that follow, Christ's ministry is shown to be superior to Aaron's because He officiates in a better sanctuary (verses 1-5) and in connection with a better covenant (verses 7-13).

The writer has now come to the chief point of his argument. He is not summarizing what has been said but stating the main thesis to which he has been leading in the Epistle.

"We have such a high priest. . . ." There is a triumphant note in the words, "we have." They are an answer to the Jewish people who taunted the early Christians with the words, "We have the Tabernacle; we have the priesthood, we have the offerings; we have the ceremonies; we have the Temple; we have the beautiful priestly garments." The believers' confident answer is, "Yes, you have the shadows but we have the Substance. You have the types but we have the fulfillment. You have the ceremonies but we have Christ. You have the pictures but we have the Person. And our High Priest is seated at the right hand of the throne of the Majesty in Heaven. No other high priest ever sat down in recognition of a finished work, and none ever held such a place of honor and of power."

8:2. He serves the people in the sanctuary of Heaven. This is the true tent, of which the earthly Tabernacle was a mere copy or representation. The true Tabernacle was divinely constructed and not erected by men, as was the earthly tent.

8:3. Since one of the principal functions of a high priest is to offer gifts and sacrifices, it follows that our High Priest must do this also.

Gifts is a general term covering all types of offerings presented to God. Sacrifices were gifts in which an animal was slain.

What does Christ offer? The question is not answered directly till we get to chapter 9.

8:4. This verse skips over the question of what Christ offers, and simply reminds us that on earth He would not be eligible to offer gifts in the Tabernacle or Temple. Our Lord was descended from Judah and not from the tribe of Levi or the family of Aaron. For this reason He was not qualified to serve in the earthly sanctuary. When we read in the Gospels that Jesus went into the Temple (see Luke 19:45), we must understand that He went only into the area surrounding it, and not into the holy place or the holy of holies.

This of course raises the question whether Christ performed any high priestly functions when He was on earth, or was it only after He ascended that He began His priestly work? The point of verse 4 is that *He was not qualified on earth as a Levitical priest, and could not serve in the Temple in Jerusalem.* But this does not mean that He could not perform the functions of *a Melchizedekan priest.* After all, His prayer in John 17 is generally conceded to be a high priestly prayer, and His offering of Himself as the one perfect sacrifice at Calvary was certainly a priestly act (see 2:17).

8:5. The Tabernacle on earth was a replica of the heavenly sanctuary. Its layout depicted the manner in which God's covenant people could approach Him in worship. First there was the door of the outer court, then the altar of burnt offering, then the laver. After that the priests entered the holy place and the high priest entered the most holy place where God manifested Himself.

The Tabernacle was never intended to be the ultimate sanctuary. It was only a copy and shadow. When God called Moses up to Mount Sinai and told him to build the Tabernacle, He gave him a definite blueprint to follow. This pattern was a type of a higher, heavenly, spiritual reality.

Why does the writer emphasize this so forcefully? Simply to impress on the minds of any who might be tempted to go back to Judaism that they were leaving the substance for the shadows when they should be going on from shadow to substance.

Verse 5 clearly teaches that Old Testament institutions were types of heavenly realities; therefore it justifies the teaching of typology when it is done in consonance with Scripture and without becoming fanciful.

8:6. This verse forms a transition between the subject of the superior sanctuary and the discussion of the superior covenant.

First, there is a comparison. Christ's ministry is as superior to the ministry of the Aaronic priests as the covenant He mediates is better than the old one.

Secondly, a reason is given: the covenant is better because it is enacted on better promises.

Christ's ministry is infinitely better. He offered Himself, not an animal. He presented the value of His own blood, not the blood of bulls and goats. He put away sins, not merely covered them. He gave believers a perfect conscience, not an annual reminder of sins. He opened the way for us to enter into the presence of God, not to stand outside at a distance.

He is the Mediator of a better covenant. As Mediator He stands between God and man to bridge the gap of estrangement. "The covenant is better because it is absolute, not conditional; spiritual, not carnal; universal,

not local; eternal, not temporal; internal, not external"
(W.H. Griffith-Thomas).

It is a better covenant because it is founded on better
promises. The covenant of law promised blessing for
obedience but threatened death for disobedience. It
required righteousness but did not give the ability to
produce it.

The new covenant is an unconditional covenant of
grace. It imputes righteousness where there is none. It
teaches men to live righteously, empowers them to do
so, and rewards them when they do.

V. *Christ's Ministry Superior to Aaron's* (8:1-13)
   (continued)
   B. *The two covenants contrasted* (8:7-13)
      1. *The first covenant*
         a. *Manifest imperfection:* For if that first
            covenant had been faultless, there would
            have been no occasion for a second.
         b. *Divine dissatisfaction:* For He finds fault
            with them when He says:
            (1) *Prospect:* "The days will come, says
                the Lord, when I will establish a new
                covenant with the house of Israel
                and with the house of Judah;
            (2) *Retrospect:* not like the covenant
                that I made with their fathers on the
                day when I took them by the hand
                to lead them out of the land of
                Egypt;
            (3) *Disobedience:* for they did not
                continue in My covenant,

(4) *Disregard:* and so I paid no heed to them, says the Lord.

2. *The new covenant:* This is the covenant that I will make with the house of Israel after those days, says the Lord:

   a. *Internal knowledge:* I will put My laws into their minds;

   b. *Inward love:* and write them on their hearts,

   c. *Priceless possession:* and I will be their God,

   d. *Privileged position:* and they shall be My people.

   e. *Universal knowledge*

      (1) *Teachers unnecessary:* And they shall not teach everyone his fellow or every one his brother, saying, 'Know the Lord,'

      (2) *Truth unrestricted:* for all shall know Me, from the least of them to the greatest.

   f. *Iniquities forgiven:* For I will be merciful toward their iniquities,

   g. *Sins forgotten:* and I will remember their sins no more."

3. *The first covenant obsolete:* In speaking of a new covenant He treats the first as obsolete. And what is becoming obsolete and growing old is ready to vanish away.

8:7. The first covenant was not perfect, that is, it was not successful in achieving an ideal relationship between man and God. It was never intended to be the final covenant, but was preparatory to the coming of Christ. The fact that another covenant is mentioned later shows that the first was not the ideal.

8:8. Actually the trouble was not with the first covenant itself: "the law is holy, and the commandment is holy and just and good" (Romans 7:12). The trouble was with the people to whom it was given; the law had poor raw materials with which to work. This is stated here in verse 8: "For He finds fault with *them* when He says. . . ." He did not find fault with the covenant but with His covenant people. The first covenant was based upon man's promise to obey (Exodus 19:8; 24:7), and therefore it was not destined to last very long. The new covenant is a recital, from beginning to end, of what God agrees to do; this is its strength.

The writer now quotes Jeremiah 31:31-34 to show that in the Jewish Scriptures God had promised a new covenant. The whole argument revolves around the word *new.* If the old was sufficient and satisfactory, why introduce a new one?

Yet God specifically promised to establish a new covenant with the house of Israel and with the house of Judah. As mentioned previously, the new covenant has to do primarily with the nation of Israel and not with the Church. It will find its complete fulfillment when Christ comes back to reign over the repentant and redeemed nation. In the meantime some of the blessings of the covenant are enjoyed by all believers. Thus when the Saviour passed the cup of wine to His disciples, He said, "This cup is the new covenant in My blood. Do this, as often as you drink it, in remembrance of Me" (1 Corinthians 11:25).

"And so we distinguish between the primary interpretation to Israel, and the secondary, spiritual application to the Church today. We now enjoy in the power of the Holy Spirit the blessings of the new covenant, and yet there will be still further and future manifestations for Israel according to God's promise" (quoted by Henderson).

8:9. God specifically promised that the new covenant would not be like the covenant which He made with them when He led them by the hand out of Egypt. How would it be different? He does not say, but perhaps the answer is implied in the remainder of the verse, "for they did not continue in My covenant, and so I paid no heed to them, says the Lord." The covenant of the law failed because it was conditional; it called for obedience from a people who did not produce it. By making the new covenant an unconditional covenant of grace, God avoids any possibility of failure since fulfillment depends on Himself alone and He cannot fail.

The quotation from Jeremiah contains a radical change. The words in Jeremiah 31:32, "though I was their husband," become in Hebrews 8:9, "so I paid no heed to them." The same Holy Spirit who inspired Jeremiah also directed the writer to the Hebrews to make the change.

8:10. Notice the repetition of the words, "I will." The old covenant tells what man must do; the new covenant tells what God will do. After the days of

Israel's disobedience are past, He will put His laws into their minds so that they will know them, and into their hearts so that they will love them. They will want to obey, not through fear of punishment but through love for Him. The laws will no longer be written in stone but on the fleshly tables of the heart.

"I will be their God, and they shall be My people." This speaks of nearness. The Old Testament told man to stand at a distance; grace tells him to come near. It also speaks of unbroken relationship and unconditional security. Nothing will ever interrupt this blood-bought tie.

8:11. The new covenant also includes universal knowledge of the Lord. During Christ's glorious reign, it will not be necessary for a man to teach his fellow citizen or his brother to know the Lord. Everyone will have an inward consciousness of Him, from the least to the greatest: "The earth shall be full of the knowledge of the Lord as the waters cover the sea" (Isaiah 11:9).

8:12. Best of all, the new covenant promises mercy for an iniquitous people and eternal forgetfulness of their sins.

There was no mercy under the law. It was inflexible and unbending: "Every transgression or disobedience received a just retribution" (Hebrews 2:2).

Furthermore, the law could not deal effectively with sins. It provided for the atonement (covering) of sins but not for their removal. Its sacrifices made a man ceremonially clean, that is, they qualified him to engage in the religious life of the nation. But this ritual cleansing was external; it did not touch a man's inward life. It did not provide moral cleansing or give him a clear conscience.

8:13. The fact that God introduces a new covenant means that the former one is obsolete. Since this is so, there should be no thought of going back to the law. Yet that is exactly what some of the professing believers were tempted to do. The author warns them that the legal covenant is outmoded; a better covenant has been introduced. They should get in step with God.

CHAPTER 9

VI. *Christ's Offering Superior to Those of the Old Testament* (9:1—10:18)

  A. *The services of the Levitical system* (9:1-10)

    1. *Ordinances for worship:* Now even the first covenant had regulations for worship

    2. *The earthly sanctuary:* and an earthly sanctuary.

      a. *First room — the holy place:* For a tent was prepared, the outer one, in which were the lampstand and the table and the bread of the Presence; it is called the Holy Place.

      b. *Second room — the holiest of all:* Behind the second curtain stood a tent called the Holy of Holies,

        (1) *Golden altar:* having the golden altar of incense

        (2) *Ark:* and the ark of the covenant

          (a) *Construction:* covered on all sides with gold,

          (b) *Contents*: which contained a golden urn holding the manna, and Aaron's rod that budded, and the tables of the covenant;

        (c) *Cover:* above it were the cherubim of glory overshadowing the mercy seat.

      (3) *Further description waived:* Of these things we cannot now speak in detail.

9:1. In the previous chapter (8:3), the writer had made passing mention of the fact that every high priest must have something to offer. He is now ready to discuss the offering of our Great High Priest and to contrast it with the Old Testament offerings. To introduce the subject he gives a rapid review of the layout of the Tabernacle and of the regulations for worship.

9:2. The Tabernacle was a tentlike structure in which God dwelt among the Israelites from the time of their encampment at Mount Sinai to the building of the Temple.

The area around the Tabernacle was called the outer court. It was enclosed by a fence consisting of a series of bronze posts with linen cloth stretched between them.

As the Israelite entered the tabernacle court through the gate at the east, he came first to the altar of burnt offering, where the sacrificial animals were slain and burned; then to the laver, a large bronze stand containing water, in which the priests washed their hands and feet.

The Tabernacle itself measured about 45 feet long, 15 feet wide, and 15 feet high. It was divided into two compartments. The first, the holy place, was 30 feet long and the second, the most holy, was 15 feet long.

The tent consisted of a wooden framework covered by goats' hair curtains and weatherproof drapes of animal skins. These coverings formed the top, back, and sides of the tent. The front of the Tabernacle was an embroidered veil.

The holy place contained three articles of furniture:

1. The table of showbread, on which were twelve cakes of bread, representing the twelve tribes of Israel. These cakes were called "bread of the Presence" because they were set before the face or presence of God.

2. The golden lampstand, with seven arms reaching upward and holding oil-burning lamps.

3. The golden altar of incense, on which holy incense was burned morning and evening.

9:3. Beyond the second veil was the most holy place or the holy of holies. Here God manifested Himself in a bright shining cloud. It was the one spot on earth where He could be approached with the blood of atonement.

9:4. This second compartment of the original Tabernacle contained the ark of the covenant, a large wooden chest overlaid with gold. Inside the chest were the golden urn holding manna, Aaron's rod that budded, and the two tables of the law. (When the Temple was erected later, there was nothing in the ark but the tables of the law — see 1 Kings 8:9).

Verse 4 says that the golden altar of incense was also in the most holy place. This presents a difficulty. In the Old Testament, this altar is assigned to the holy place (Exodus 30:6). The best explanation is that this altar was regarded as belonging to the most holy place because it was placed immediately opposite the ark with only the veil between.

9:5. The gold lid of the ark of the covenant was known as the mercy seat. On top of it were two golden angelic figures known as cherubim. They faced each other, with wings overspread, and with heads bowed over the cover of the ark.

The writer stops with this brief description. It is not his purpose to go into great detail, but merely to outline the contents of the Tabernacle and the way of approach to God which it depicted.

VI. *Christ's Offering Superior to Those of the Old Testament* (9:1—10:18) *(continued)*
   A. *The services of the Levitical system* (9:1-10) *(continued)*
      3. *The prescribed ritual*
         a. *Sphere of the priest:* These preparations having thus been made, the priests go continually into the outer tent, performing their ritual duties;
         b. *Sphere of the high priest*
            (1) *Solitary man:* but into the second only the high priest goes,
            (2) *Single day:* and he but once a year,
            (3) *Sin-atoning blood:* and not without taking blood which he offers for himself and for the errors of the people.
         c. *Symbolic meaning*
            (1) *Teacher:* By this the Holy Spirit indicates

      (2) *Teaching:* that the way into the sanctuary is not yet opened

      (3) *Term:* while as yet the first tabernacle has [its] standing (JND);

      (4) *Typology:* (which is symbolic for the present age).

   d. *Spiritual appraisal*

      (1) *Powerless to perfect:* According to this arrangement, gifts and sacrifices are offered which cannot perfect the conscience of the worshiper,

      (2) *Dealing with defilement:* but deal only with food and drink and various ablutions,

      (3) *Temporary in tenure:* regulations for the body imposed until the time of reformation.

9:6. Since the writer is going to contrast Christ's offering with the offerings of Judaism, he must first of all describe those which were required by the law. There were many he could choose from, but he selects the most important in the whole legal system, the sacrifice which was offered on the great Day of Atonement (Leviticus 16). If he can prove Christ's work to be superior to that of the high priest on the outstanding day of Israel's religious calendar, then he has won his point.

The priests had access to the outer tent, that is, the holy place. They went there continually in the performance of their ritual duties. The common people were not permitted in this room; they had to stay outside.

9:7. Only one man in the world could go into the most holy place — the high priest of Israel. And that one man, out of one race, out of one tribe, out of one family could enter on only one day of the year — the Day of Atonement. When he did enter, he was required to carry a basin of blood which he offered for himself and for the errors of the people.

9:8. There were deep spiritual truths connected with this. The Holy Spirit was teaching that sin had created distance between man and God, that man must approach God through a mediator, and that the mediator could approach God only through the blood of a sacrificial victim. It was an object lesson to teach that the way into God's presence was not yet opened for worshipers.

Imperfect access continued, according to the RSV, "as long as the outer tent was still standing." But Darby's translation seems preferable here: "while as yet the first tabernacle has [its] standing." The Tabernacle was displaced by the Temple during the reign of Solomon, but it still had a standing until the death, burial, and resurrection of Christ. The principles it proclaimed concerning approach to God were still valid until the veil of the Temple was rent in two from the top to the bottom.

9:9. The tabernacle system is symbolic for the present age. A picture of something better to come, it was an imperfect representation of Christ's perfect work.

Its gifts and offerings could never make the worshipers perfect as to their consciences. If complete remission of sins had been procured, then the offerer's conscience would have been free from the guilt of sin. But this never happened.

9:10. As a matter of fact, the Levitical offerings dealt only with ritual defilement. They were concerned with such externals as clean and unclean food and drink, and with ceremonial cleansings that would rid the people of ritual impurity, but they did not deal with moral uncleanness.

The offerings were concerned with a people who were in covenant relationship with God. They were designed to maintain the people in a position of ritual purity so that they could worship. They had nothing to do with salvation or with cleansing from sin. The people were saved by faith in the Lord, on the basis of the work of Christ still future.

Finally the sacrifices were temporary. They were imposed until the time of reformation. They pointed forward to the coming of Christ and to His perfect offering. The Christian era is the time of reformation referred to here.

VI. *Christ's Offering Superior to Those of the Old Testament* (9:1—10:18) *(continued)*

    B. *The surpassing service of Christ* (9:11-14)

        1. *The superlative High Priest:* But when Christ appeared as a high priest of the good things that have come,

        2. *The superior Tabernacle:* then through the

greater and more perfect tent (not made with hands, that is, not of this creation)

3. *The sublime entrance:* He entered once for all into the Holy Place,

4. *The singular offering:* taking not the blood of goats and calves but His own blood,

5. *The secured redemption:* thus securing an eternal redemption.

6. *A subordinate cleansing*
   (1) *Persons affected:* For if the sprinkling of defiled persons
   (2) *Means applied:* with the blood of goats and bulls and with the ashes of a heifer
   (3) *Results achieved:* sanctifies for the purification of the flesh,

7. *The supreme cleansing*
   (1) *The cleansing agent:* how much more shall the blood of Christ,
   (2) *The enabling Power:* who through the eternal Spirit
   (3) *The spotless offering:* offered Himself without blemish to God,
   (4) *The matchless efficacy:* purify your conscience from dead works
   (5) *The resulting freedom:* to serve the living God.

9:11. Christ has appeared as a High Priest of the good things that have come, that is, of the tremendous blessings that He has bestowed on those who receive Him.

His sanctuary is a greater and more perfect tent. It is not made with hands in the sense that it is not constructed of this world's building materials. It is the sanctuary of Heaven, the dwelling place of God.

> No temple made with hands,
>   His place of service is;
> In Heaven itself He serves,
>   A heavenly priesthood His:
> In him the shadows of the law
>   Are all fulfilled, and now withdraw.

9:12. Our Lord entered once for all into the holy place. At the time of His ascension, He went into God's presence, having finished the work of redemption at Calvary. We should never cease to rejoice over those words, "once for all." The work is completed. Praise the Lord!

He offered His own blood, not the blood of bulls and goats. Animal blood had no power to put away sins; it was effective only in cases of technical offenses against religious ritual. But the blood of Christ is of infinite value; its power is sufficient to cleanse all the sins of all the people who have ever lived, all the people who are living, and all the people who will ever live. Of course, its power is applicable only to those who come to Him by faith. But its cleansing potential is unlimited.

By His sacrifice He obtained eternal redemption. The former priests obtained annual atonement. There is a vast difference between the two.

9:13. To illustrate the difference between the sacrifice of Christ and the ceremonies of the law, the writer now turns to the ritual of the red heifer. Under the law, if an Israelite touched a dead man, he became ceremonially unclean for seven days. The remedy was to mix the ashes of a red heifer with pure spring water and to sprinkle the defiled person on the third and seventh days. He then became clean.

Mantle says that "the ashes were regarded as a concentration of the essential properties of the sin offering, and could be resorted to at all times with comparatively little trouble and no loss of time. One red heifer availed for centuries. Only six are said to have been required during the whole of Jewish history; for the smallest quantity of the ashes availed to impart the cleansing virtue to the pure spring water (Numbers 19:17)."

9:14. If the ashes of a heifer had such power to cleanse from one of the most serious forms of outward defilement, how much more powerful is the blood of Christ to cleanse from inward sins of deepest dye.

His offering was "through the eternal Spirit." There is some difference of opinion as to the meaning of this expression. Some interpret it to mean, "Through an eternal spirit," meaning the willing spirit in which He made His sacrifice in contrast to the involuntary character of animal offerings. Others understand it to mean, "Through His eternal spirit." We rather believe that the Holy Spirit is in view; He made His sacrifice in the power of the Holy Spirit.

It was an offering without blemish to God. He was the sinless, spotless Lamb of God whose moral perfection qualified Him to be our Sin-bearer. The animal sacrifices had to be physically spotless; He was without blemish morally.

His blood purges the conscience from dead works to serve the living God. It is not merely a physical purging or a ceremonial cleansing but a moral renewal that purifies the conscience. It cleanses from those dead works which unbelievers produce in an effort to earn their own cleansing. It frees men from these lifeless works to serve the living God.

VI. *Christ's Offering Superior to Those of the Old Testament* (9:1−10:18) *(continued)*

    C. *The sacrificial death of Christ and its ratification of the new covenant* (9:15-22)

        1. *Promised inheritance received:* Therefore He is the mediator of a new covenant, so that those who are called may receive the promised eternal inheritance,

        2. *Pretermission of sins procured:* since a death has occurred which redeems them from the transgressions under the first covenant.

        3. *Parallel in the case of a last will:* For where a will is involved, the death of the one who made it must be established. For a will takes effect only at death, since it is not in force as long as the one who made it is alive.

        4. *Parallel in the case of the old covenant:* Hence even the first covenant was not ratified without blood.

            a. *The reading of the law:* For when every commandment of the law had been declared by Moses to all the people,

> b. *The ratifying blood:* he took the blood
>   of calves and goats, with water and
>   scarlet wool and hyssop,
> c. *The contracting parties:* and sprinkled
>   both the book itself and all the people,
> d. *The ratifying formula:* saying, "This is
>   the blood of the covenant which God
>   commanded you."
> e. *The sprinkled sanctuary:* And in the
>   same way he sprinkled with the blood
>   both the tent and all the vessels used in
>   worship.
>
> 5. *Principles of purification under the law*
>   a. *Most things cleansed by blood:* Indeed,
>   under the law almost everything is
>   purified with blood,
>   b. *Sins forgiven only by blood:* and with-
>   out the shedding of blood there is no
>   forgiveness of sins.

9:15. The previous verses stressed the superiority of
the blood of the new covenant to the blood of the old.
This leads to the conclusion of verse 15 — that Christ is
the Mediator of a new covenant. "The word 'mediator'
is the translation of *mesites* which refers to one who
intervenes between two, to make or restore peace and
friendship, to form a compact, or to ratify a covenant.
Here the Messiah acts as a go-between or mediator
between a holy God and sinful man. By His death on
the cross, He removes the obstacle (sin) which caused an
estrangement between man and God. When the sinner

accepts the merits of Messiah's sacrifice, the guilt and penalty of his sin is his no more, the power of sin in his life is broken, he becomes the recipient of the divine nature, and the estrangement between himself and God, both legal and personal, disappears" (Wuest).

Now those who are called may receive the promised eternal inheritance. Through Christ's work saints of the Old Testament as well as of the New enjoy eternal salvation and eternal redemption.

The fact that qualifies believers of the pre-Christian era for the inheritance is that a death has occurred, that is, the death of Christ. His death redeems them from transgressions under the law.

There is a sense in which God saved Old Testament people on credit. They were justified by faith, just as we are. But Christ had not died as yet. Then how could God save them? The answer is that He saved them on the basis of what He knew Christ would accomplish. They knew little or nothing of what Christ would do at Calvary. But God knew, and He reckoned the value of that work to their account when they believed whatever revelation He gave them of Himself.

In a sense a great debt of transgression had accumulated under the old covenant. By His death, Christ redeemed believers of the former dispensation from these transgressions.

The manner in which God saved them through the still-future work of Christ is known as the pretermission of sins. It is discussed in Romans 3:25-26.

9:16. The author's mention of inheritance in verse 15 reminds him that before a last will and testament can be probated, evidence must be submitted that the testator has died. Usually a death certificate is sufficient evidence.

9:17. The testator may have drawn up his will many years previously and kept it secure in his safe, but it does not take effect until he dies. As long as he is alive, his property cannot be distributed to those named in the will.

9:18. Now the subject switches from a person's last will to the old testament given by God through Moses. Here too a death had to take place. It was ratified by the shedding of blood.

In olden times every covenant was made valid by the sacrificial death of an animal. The blood was a pledge that the terms of the covenant would be fulfilled.

9:19. After Moses had recited the laws to Israel he took:

> the blood of calves and goats
> water
> scarlet wool
> hyssop

and sprinkled

> the book of the law
> all the people.

(In the account in Exodus 24, we find no mention of any of these except the blood and the people.)

Thus Moses arranged the ceremony for the solemn sealing of the covenant (Exodus 24:1-11). The altar symbolized God's presence. With half the blood of the animals the patriarch sprinkled the altar and with the other half, the people. This indicated that both contracting parties bound themselves to keep the terms of the covenant. The people promised to obey, and Jehovah promised to bless them if they did obey.

9:20. As he sprinkled the blood he said, "This is the blood of the covenant which God commanded you." This action pledged the life of the people if they failed to keep the law.

9:21. In a similar manner Moses sprinkled with blood the Tabernacle and all the vessels used in worship. This ritual is not found in the Old Testament. No mention is made of blood in the consecration of the Tabernacle in Exodus 40. However, the symbolism is clear. Everything that has any contact with sinful man becomes defiled and needs to be cleansed.

9:22. Almost everything under the law was cleansed by blood. But there were exceptions. For instance, when a man was to be numbered in a census among the children of Israel, he could bring a half-shekel of silver as "atonement money" instead of a blood offering (Exodus 30:11-16). The coin was a token symbolizing atonement for the man's soul in order for him to be reckoned as one of God's people. Another exception is found in Leviticus 5:11, where certain forms of ritual uncleanness could be dealt with by an offering of fine flour.

These exceptions dealt with *atonement* for or *covering* of sin, although generally speaking a blood offering was required even for atonement. But as far as *remission* of sin is concerned, there is no exception; blood must be shed.

VI. *Christ's Offering Superior to Those of the Old Testament* (9:1—10:18) *(continued)*

D. *Similarities and contrasts between the two covenants* (9:23-28)

1. *Cleansing of the sanctuary and vessels*

   a. *The earthly types:* Thus it was necessary for the copies of the heavenly things to be purified with these rites,

   b. *The heavenly realities:* but the heavenly things themselves with better sacrifices than these.

2. *The entrance of the priest*

   a. *Pattern sanctuary:* For Christ has entered, not into a sanctuary made with hands, a copy of the true one,

   b. *Present location:* but into heaven itself,

   c. *Priestly function:* now to appear in the presence of God

   d. *Personal representation:* on our behalf.

3. *The offerings*

   a. *The old covenant*

      (1) *Intermittent oblations:* Nor was it to offer Himself repeatedly,

      (2) *Inferior blood:* as the high priest enters the Holy Place yearly with blood not his own;

      (3) *Incessant suffering:* for then He would have had to suffer repeatedly since the foundation of the world.

   b. *The new covenant*

      (1) *Positive finality:* But as it is, He has appeared once for all

    (2) *Propitious time:* at the end of the age

    (3) *Perfect work:* to put away sin

    (4) *Personal sacrifice:* by the sacrifice of Himself.

c. *The old covenant*

    (1) *Inevitable appointment:* And just as it is appointed for men to die once,

    (2) *Inescapable judgment:* and after that comes judgment,

d. *The new covenant*

    (1) *Infinite sacrifice:* so Christ, having been offered once to bear the sins of many,

    (2) *Imminent appearance:* will appear a second time,

        (a) *Not bearing sin:* not to deal with sin

        (b) *But bringing salvation:* but to save those who are eagerly waiting for Him.

9:23. In the remaining verses of the chapter the writer compares and contrasts the two covenants.

First of all, the earthly Tabernacle had to be cleansed with the blood of bulls and goats. As has been pointed out this was a ceremonial purification. It was a symbolic sanctification of a symbolic sanctuary.

The heavenly sanctuary was the reality of which the earthly tent was a copy. It has to be cleansed with better sacrifices than these, that is, with the sacrifice of Christ. The use of the plural to describe the single offering of Christ is a figure of speech known as the plural of majesty.

It may seem surprising that the heavenly places needed to be cleansed. Perhaps a clue is found in Job 15:15, "the heavens are not clean in His sight." Doubtless this is because Satan committed the first act of sin in Heaven (Isaiah 14:12-14), and because he still has access to the presence of God as the accuser of the brethren (Revelation 12:10).

9:24. Christ did not enter into the man-made sanctuary, which was a pattern or figure of the true one, but into Heaven itself. There He appears in God's presence for us.

It is difficult to understand why anyone would want to leave the reality and go back to the copy, why anyone would leave the Great High Priest serving in the heavenly sanctuary to return to the priests of Israel serving in a symbolic tent.

9:25. The Lord Jesus did not make repeated offerings, as the Aaronic high priests had to do. They went into the holy place (here meaning the most holy place) on one day of every year — that is, the Day of Atonement, and they did not offer their own blood but the blood of sacrificial animals.

9:26. If Christ had made repeated offerings, that would have meant repeated suffering, since His offering was His own life. It is unthinkable that He should have suffered the agonies of Calvary periodically since the foundation of the world! And unnecessary too!

Under the new covenant, there is:

1. Positive finality — He has appeared once for all.

The work never needs to be repeated.

2. A propitious time — He appeared at the end of the age, that is, after the old covenant had conclusively demonstrated man's failure and powerlessness.

3. A perfect work — He appeared to put away sin. The emphasis is on the words "put away." It was no longer a matter of annual atonement. Now it was eternal forgiveness.

4. A personal sacrifice — He put away sin by the sacrifice of Himself. In His own body He bore the punishment which our sins deserved.

> In my place condemned He stood;
> Sealed my pardon with His blood;
> Hallalujah! What a Saviour!

9:27. Verses 27 and 28 seem to present another contrast between the old covenant and the new. The law condemned sinners to die, and after that the judgment. It was given to a people who were already sinners and who could not keep it perfectly. Therefore it became a ministry of condemnation to all who were under it.

9:28. The new covenant introduces the infinite sacrifice of Christ; He was once offered to bear the sins of many. It presents the blessed hope of His imminent return; to those who look for Him, He will appear a second time. But when He returns, it will not be to deal with the problem of sin: He finished that work at the cross. He will come to take His people home to Heaven. This will be the culmination of their salvation; they will receive their glorified bodies and be forever beyond the reach of sin.

The expression, "those who are eagerly waiting for Him," is a description of all true believers. All the Lord's people look for Him to return, though they may not agree on the exact order of events connected with His coming.

The Bible does not teach that only a certain group of especially spiritual Christians will be taken to Heaven at the time of the rapture. It describes the participants as "the dead in Christ" and "we who are alive, who are left" (1 Thessalonians 4:16-17); this means all true believers, dead or living. In 1 Corinthians 15:23 the participants are identified as "those who belong to Christ."

It has often been pointed out that we have three appearances of Christ in verses 24-28. They may be summarized as follows:

Verse 26 — He has appeared — this refers to His first advent when He came to earth to save us from the penalty of sin (the past tense of salvation).

Verse 24 — He now appears — a reference to His present ministry in the presence of God to save us from the power of sin (the present tense of salvation).

Verse 28 — He will appear — His imminent return when He will save us from the presence of sin (the future tense of salvation).

CHAPTER 10

VI. *Christ's Offering Superior to Those of the Old Testament* (9:1–10:18) *(continued)*
   E. *The weakness of the law* (10:1-4)
      1. *A shadow:* For since the law has but a shadow of the good things to come
      2. *Not substance:* instead of the true form of these realities,
      3. *Its sacrifices*
         a. *Multiple:* it can never, by the same sacrifices
         b. *Continual:* which are continually offered
         c. *Annual:* year after year,
         d. *Ineffectual:* [can never] make perfect those who draw near.
            (1) *Question:* Otherwise, would they not have ceased to be offered?
            (2) *Answer:* If the worshipers had once been cleansed, they would no longer have any consciousness of sin.
         e. *Memorial:* But in these sacrifices there is a reminder of sin year after year.
         f. *Incapable:* For it is impossible that the blood of bulls and goats should take away sins.

10:1. The law was only a shadow of the good things that were to come. It pointed forward to the Person and work of Christ but it was a poor substitute for the reality. To prefer the law to Christ is like preferring a picture to the person represented. It is an insult to Him.

The weakness of the legal system is seen in the fact that its sacrifices had to be constantly repeated. This repetition proved their total inability to meet the claims of a holy God. Notice the expressions used to capture this idea of repetitiveness: the same sacrifice — continually offered — year after year.

The sacrifices were utterly unable to perfect the worshipers, that is, they never gave the people a perfect conscience as far as sin was concerned. The Israelites never enjoyed the consciousness of being cleared forever from the guilt of sin. They never had complete rest of conscience.

10:2. If the offerings had completely and finally absolved them from sin, then they could have ceased making the annual trek to the Tabernacle or Temple. The regular recurrence of the sacrifices branded them as ineffectual. "He who is obliged to take medicine every hour to keep life in him cannot be said to be cured" (Govett).

10:3. Instead of pacifying the conscience, the Levitical system stabbed it awake each year. Behind the beautiful ritual of the Day of Atonement lurked the constant reminder that sins were only being covered, not removed.

10:4. The blood of bulls and goats simply did not have the power to take away sins. As mentioned previously, these sacrifices dealt with ritual errors. They gave a certain ceremonial cleansing but they were utter failures as far as providing satisfaction for man's corrupt nature or for his evil deeds.

VI. *Christ's Offering Superior to Those of the Old Testament* (9:1–10:18) *(continued)*
   F. *The superlative sacrifice of Christ* (10:5-18)
      1. *His incarnation soliloquy*: Consequently, when Christ came into the world, He said,
         a. *God's dissatisfaction:* "Sacrifices and offerings Thou hast not desired,
         b. *God's design:* but a body hast Thou prepared for Me;
         c. *God's displeasure:* in burnt offerings and sin offerings Thou hast taken no pleasure.
         d. *Christ's dedication*
            (1) *Personal submission:* Then I said, 'Lo, I have come to do Thy will, O God,'
            (2) *Scriptural affirmation:* as it is written of Me in the roll of the book."
      2. *The spiritual significance of the soliloquy*
         a. *Imperfection:* When He said above, "Thou hast neither desired nor taken pleasure in sacrifices and offerings and burnt offerings and sin offerings" (these are offered according to the law),
         b. *Perfection:* then He added, "Lo, I have come to do Thy will."
         c. *Abolition:* He abolishes the first

    d. *Ratification:* in order to establish the second.

      (1) *God's will:* And by that will

      (2) *Our sanctification:* we have been sanctified

      (3) *Christ's offering:* through the offering of the body of Jesus Christ once for all.

10:5. In contrast to the weakness of the Levitical offerings, we come now to the strength of the superlative sacrifice of Christ. By way of introduction, we are permitted to hear the Saviour's soliloquy at the time of His incarnation. Quoting from Psalm 40, He noted God's dissatisfaction with the sacrifices and offerings of the old covenant. God had instituted these sacrifices, yet they were never His ultimate intention. They were never designed to put away sins but rather to point forward to the Lamb of God who would bear away the sin of the world. Could God be pleased with rivers of animal blood or with heaps of animal carcasses?

Another reason for God's dissatisfaction is that the people thought they were pleasing Him by going through ceremonies while their inward lives were sinful and corrupt. Most of them went through the dreary round of sacrifices with no repentance or contrition. They thought that God could be appeased with their animal sacrifices whereas He was looking for the sacrifice of a broken heart. They did not realize that God is not a ritualist!

Dissatisfied with the former sacrifices, God prepared

a human body for His Son which was an integral part of His human life and nature. This, of course, refers to the unfathomable wonder of the Incarnation when the eternal Word became flesh so that, as Man, He might die for men.

It is interesting that the clause, "a body hast Thou prepared for Me," adapted from Psalm 40:6, is capable of two other meanings. In that Psalm it reads, "Thou hast given Me an open ear," and in the margin it says, "ears Thou hast dug for Me." The open ear, of course, signifies that the Messiah was always ready to receive His instructions from God and to obey them instantly. The dug ear may be an allusion to the Hebrew slave (Exodus 21:1-6), whose ear was bored with an awl to the door as a sign that he willingly indentured himself to his master forever. In His incarnation, the Saviour said, in effect, "I love My Master . . . I will not go out free."

10:6. Continuing the quotation from Psalm 40, the Lord Jesus repeated that God took no pleasure in burnt offerings and sin offerings. The animals were unwilling victims whose blood was powerless to cleanse.

10:7. What did bring pleasure to God was the Messiah's willingness to do God's will, no matter what the cost might be. He proved His willing obedience by offering Himself on the altar of sacrifice.

As our Lord uttered those words, He was reminded that from the beginning to the end of the Old Testament Scriptures, it is witnessed of Him that He took wholehearted delight in accomplishing the will of God. (The Scriptures at that time were in the form of a scroll; hence the reference to the roll of the book.)

10:8. In verses 8-10 the writer gives the spiritual significance of the soliloquy. He sees it as signaling the demise of the old sacrificial system and the inauguration of the one perfect, complete, and final offering of Jesus Christ.

He repeats the quotation from Psalm 40 in condensed form to emphasize God's displeasure with the sacrifices that were offered according to the law.

10:9. Then the writer sees significance in the fact that immediately after declaring God's displeasure with the old, the Messiah stepped forward, as it were, to do the thing that *would* please the heart of His Father.

The conclusion: He abolishes the first to establish the second, that is, He takes away the old system of offerings that were required by law, and introduces His own great sacrifice for sin. The legal covenant retires to the wings of the stage as the new covenant moves to the center.

10:10. By that will of God, to which Jesus was utterly obedient, we have been sanctified through the offering of the body of Jesus Christ once for all. "This is a positional sanctification, as is the case all through Hebrews with the exception of 12:14, and is true of all believers (1 Corinthians 6:11) and not merely of a few 'advanced Christians.' It is accomplished by the will of God and the sacrifice of Christ. We are set apart *by* God, *to* God, and *for* God. It is not to be confused with the progressive work of God's Spirit in the believer through the Word (John 17:17-19; 1 Thessalonians 5:23)" (Landis).

VI. *Christ's Offering Superior to Those of the Old Testament* (9:1—10:18) *(continued)*

   F. *The superlative sacrifice of Christ* (10:5-18) *(continued)*

      3. *The first and second systems contrasted*

         a. *The ministry of the priests*

            (1) *Daily posture:* And every priest stands daily at his service,

            (2) *Continual offerings:* offering repeatedly the same sacrifices,

            (3) *Discouraging result:* which can never take away sins.

         b. *The ministry of the Lord Jesus*

            (1) *Final offering:* But when Christ had offered for all time

            (2) *Single sacrifice:* a single sacrifice for sins,

            (3) *Eternal posture:* He sat down

            (4) *Honored place:* at the right hand of God,

            (5) *Resulting prospect:* then to wait until His enemies should be made a stool for His feet.

            (6) *Glorious result*

               (a) *One offering:* For by a single offering

               (b) *Eternal efficacy:* He has perfected for all time

               (c) *Satisfied saints:* those who are sanctified.

    c. *The witness of the Holy Spirit*
       (1) *New covenant promised:* And the Holy Spirit also bears witness to us; for after saying,
          (a) *Divine assurance:* "This is the covenant that I will make with them after those days, says the Lord:
          (b) *Loving obedience:* I will put My laws on their hearts,
          (c) *Constant remembrance:* and write them on their minds,"
       (2) *Full forgiveness guaranteed:* then He adds, "I will remember their sins and their misdeeds no more."
       (3) *Further sacrifice unnecessary:* Where there is forgiveness of these, there is no longer any offering for sin.

10:11. The ministry of the Aaronic priests is now contrasted sharply with that of Christ. The former stood daily in the performance of their duties. There was no chair in the Tabernacle or Temple. There could be no rest because their work was never completed. They repeatedly offered the same sacrifices. It was an unending routine which left sins untouched and the conscience unrelieved.

The sacrifices could never take away sins. "Aaron, though an important personage within the Levitical system, was after all but a sacerdotal drudge, ever performing ceremonies which had no real value" (Bruce).

10:12. Our blessed Lord offered a single sacrifice for sin. None other would ever be needed!

> No blood, no altar now,
> The sacrifice is o'er!
> No flame, no smoke ascends on high,
> The lamb is slain no more.
> But richer blood has flowed
> From nobler veins
> To purge the soul from guilt
> And cleanse the reddest stains.
> —Horatius Bonar

Having finished the work of redemption, He "sat down in perpetuity at [the] right hand of God" (JND). There is a difference of opinion among Bible students whether the verse means that He offered a single sacrifice for sins forever, or that He sat down forever. Both are true, but we tend to believe that the latter is the correct interpretation. He is seated uninterruptedly because sin's tremendous claim has been settled forever. He is seated at the right hand of God, the place of honor, power, and affection.

> He fills the throne, the throne above,
> He fills it without wrong;
> The object of His Father's love,
> The theme of Heaven's song.
> —Thomas Kelly

Perhaps someone will object that He cannot be seated forever since He will one day rise in judgment. There is no contradiction here, however. As far as making an offering for sin is concerned, He has sat down in perpetuity. As far as judgment is concerned, He is not seated forever.

10:13. He waits till His enemies will be made His footstool, till the day when every knee will bow to Him, and every tongue will acknowledge Him as Lord to the glory of God the Father (Philippians 2:10-11). This will be the day of His public vindication on earth.

10:14. The surpassing value of His sacrifice is seen in that by it He has perfected forever or in perpetuity those who are sanctified. "Those who are sanctified" here means all who have been set apart to God from the world, that is, all true believers. They have been perfected in a twofold sense. First, they have a perfect standing before God; they stand before the Father in all the acceptability of His beloved Son. Secondly, they have a perfect conscience as far as the guilt and penalty of sin are concerned; they know that the price has been paid in full and that God will not demand payment a second time.

10:15. The Holy Spirit witnesses to the fact that under the new covenant, sins would be effectively dealt with once and for all. He witnesses to it through the Old Testament Scriptures.

10:16. In Jeremiah 31:31, God promised to make a new covenant with His chosen earthly people.

10:17. Then in the very same passage, He said, "I will remember their sins and their misdeeds no more" (see Jeremiah 31:34). It is arresting that the Jewish Scriptures contained this promise of full and final forgiveness of sins; yet some of those who lived in the day when the promise began to be fulfilled were disposed to return to the never-ending sacrifices of Judaism.

10:18. The promise of forgiveness under the new

covenant means that there is no longer any offering for sin. With these words, *"no longer any offering for sin,"* the author closes what we might call the doctrinal portion of the Epistle. He wants to have these words ringing in our hearts and minds as he now presses upon us our practical obligations.

VII. *Exhortations and Warnings* (10:19–13:17)
   A. *Draw near* (10:19-22)
      1. *We have great confidence:* Therefore, brethren, since we have confidence to enter the sanctuary
         a. *A blood-sprinkled way:* by the blood of Jesus,
         b. *A new and living way:* by the new and living way which He opened for us through the curtain, that is, through His flesh,
      2. *We have a great Priest:* and since we have a great priest over the house of God,
      3. *We should draw near:* let us draw near
         a. *Sincere:* with a true heart
         b. *Sure:* in full assurance of faith,
         c. *Saved:* with our hearts sprinkled clean from an evil conscience
         d. *Sanctified:* and our bodies washed with pure water.
   B. *Hold fast:* (10:23)
      1. *Confession:* Let us hold fast the confession of our hope
      2. *Constancy:* without wavering,

    3. *Certainty:* for He who promised is faithful;

C. *Stir up* (10:24): and let us consider how to stir up one another

    1. *The root:* to love

    2. *The fruit:* and good works,

D. *Neglect not* (10:25)

    1. *Continual attendance:* not neglecting to meet together,

    2. *Habitual absenteeism:* as is the habit of some,

    3. *Mutual exhortation:* but encouraging one another,

    4. *Crucial motivation:* and all the more as you see the Day drawing near.

10:19. In Old Testament times the people were kept at a distance; now in Christ we are brought near through the blood of His cross. Therefore we are encouraged to draw near.

This exhortation assumes that all believers are now priests because we are told to have boldness to enter into the holiest by the blood of Jesus. The common people during the Jewish economy were barred from the holy place and the most holy place; only the priests could enter the first room, and only the high priest could enter the second. Now that is all changed. God has no special place where only a special caste of men may approach Him. Instead, all believers may enter into His presence by faith at any time and from any place on earth.

Through the vail God bids me enter
By the new and living way;
Not in trembling hope I venture –
Boldly I His call obey;
There, with Christ my God, I meet
God upon the mercy-seat!

O the welcome I have found there,
God in all His love made known!
O the glory that surrounds there
Those accepted in His Son!
Who can tell the depths of bliss
Spoken by the Father's kiss?

All His joy told out unhindered,
Nought but Christ His eye can see;
Christ into His joy has entered,
And in Christ He welcomes me:
Would I know how dear to God?
Priceless as Christ's precious blood!

All the worth I have before Him
Is the value of the blood:
I present, when I adore Him
Christ, the First-fruits, unto God.
Him with joy doth God behold;
Thus is my acceptance told!

Place of glory, place of blessing,
Place where God His heart displays!
All in Thee, O Christ, possessing,
Thine the voice that leads our praise!
Thine the new eternal song,
Through the ages borne along!
                              Author unknown

10:20. Our approach is by the new and living way. "New" here may have the meaning of "newly slain" or "newly made." "Living" seems to be a reference to Jesus in resurrection, therefore, to a living Saviour. This way was opened through the veil, that is, His flesh. This clearly teaches that the veil between the two compartments of the Tabernacle was a type of the body of our Lord. In order for us to have access into God's presence, the veil had to be rent, that is, His body had to be broken in death. This reminds us that we cannot draw near by Christ's sinless life, but only by His vicarious death. "We enter only through the death wounds of the Lamb." Each time we enter God's presence in prayer or worship, may we remember that the privilege was purchased for us at tremendous cost.

10:21. We not only have great confidence when we enter the presence of God; we also have a great Priest over the house of God. Even though we are priests (1 Peter 2:9; Revelation 1:6), yet we still need a Priest ourselves. Christ is our great High Priest, and His present ministry for us assures our continued welcome before God.

10:22. "Let us draw near." This is the believer's blood-bought privilege. How wonderful beyond all words that we are invited to have audience, not with this world's celebrities, but with the Sovereign of the universe. The extent to which we value the invitation is shown by the manner in which we respond to it.

There is a fourfold description of how we should be spiritually groomed in entering the throne room.

> 1. "With a true heart." The people of Israel drew near to God with their mouth, and honored Him with their lips, but their heart was far from Him (Matthew 15:8). Our approach should be with utter sincerity.

2. "In full assurance of faith." We draw near with utter confidence in the promises of God and with the firm conviction that we shall have a gracious reception.

3. "With our hearts sprinkled clean from an evil conscience." This can be brought about only by the new birth. When we trust Christ, we appropriate the value of His blood. Figuratively speaking, we sprinkle our hearts with it, just as the Israelites sprinkled their doors with the blood of the passover lamb. This delivers us from an evil conscience; our testimony is:

> Conscience now no more condemns us,
> For His own most precious blood
> Once for all has washed and cleansed us,
> Cleansed us in the eyes of God.
>
> — Frances Bevan

4. "And our bodies washed with pure water." Again this is symbolic language. Our bodies represent our lives. The pure water might refer either to the Word (Ephesians 5:25-26), to the Holy Spirit (John 7:37-39), or to the Holy Spirit using the Word in cleansing our lives from daily defilement. We are cleansed once for all from the guilt of sin by the death of Christ, but cleansed repeatedly from the defilement of sin by the Spirit through the Word (see John 13:10).

Thus we might summarize the four requisites for

entering God's presence as sincerity, assurance, salvation, and sanctification.

10:23. The second exhortation is to hold fast the confession of our hope. Nothing must be allowed to turn us from the staunch confession that our only hope is in Christ.

For those who were tempted to give up the future, unseen blessings of Christianity for the present, visible things of Judaism, there is the reminder that He who promised is faithful. His promises can never fail; no one who trusts in Him will ever be disappointed. The Saviour will come, as He has promised, and His people will be with Him and like Him forever.

10:24. We should also be discovering ways of encouraging fellow believers to manifest love and to engage in good works. In the New Testament sense, love is not an unpredictable emotion but an act of the will. We are commanded to love, therefore it is something we can and must do. Love manifests itself in giving; it gives itself for others. Love is the root; good works are the fruit. By our example and by our teaching, we should stir up other believers to this kind of a life.

10:25. Then we should continue to meet together and not desert the local fellowship, as some do. This may be considered as a general exhortation for all believers to be faithful in their church attendance. Without question we find strength, comfort, nourishment, and joy in collective worship and service.

It may also be looked on as a special encouragement for Christians going through times of persecution. There is always the temptation to isolate oneself in order to avoid arrest, reproach, and suffering and thus be a secret disciple.

But basically the verse is a warning against apostasy. To forsake the local assembly here means to turn one's back on Christianity and revert to Judaism. Some were doing this when this letter was written. There was need to exhort one another, especially in view of the nearness of Christ's return. When He comes, the persecuted, ostracized, despised believers will be seen to be on the winning side. Till then, there is need for steadfastness.

VII. *Exhortations   and   Warnings*   (10:19—13:17) *(continued)*

    E. *The fourth warning — the willful sin of apostasy* (10:26-31)

       1. *Presumption:* For if we sin deliberately

       2. *Privilege:* after receiving the knowledge of the truth,

       3. *Prospect*

          a. *Forfeited forgiveness:* there no longer remains a sacrifice for sins,

          b. *Fearful judgment:* but a fearful prospect of judgment,

          c. *Furious fire:* and a fury of fire which will consume the adversaries.

       4. *The doom of the law-breaker*

          a. *Sin:* A man who has violated the law of Moses

          b. *Sentence:* dies

    c. *Severity:* without mercy

    d. *Sufficient evidence:* at the testimony of two or three witnesses.

  5. *The doom of the apostate*

    a. *His greater punishment:* How much worse punishment do you think will be deserved by the man

    b. *His sin*

      (1) *The Son spurned:* who has spurned the Son of God,

      (2) *The blood profaned:* and profaned the blood of the covenant by which he was sanctified,

      (3) *The Spirit insulted:* and outraged the Spirit of grace?

    c. *His Judge*

      (1) *Justice inexorable:* For we know Him who said, "Vengeance is Mine,

      (2) *Repayment inevitable:* I will repay."

      (3) *Judgment inescapable*: And again, "The Lord will judge His people."

      (4) *Punishment indescribable:* It is a fearful thing to fall into the hands of the living God.

10:26. Now the writer introduces his fourth grim warning. As in the previous cases, it is a warning against apostasy, here described as a deliberate sin.

As has been indicated, there is considerable disagreement among Christians as to the real nature of this sin. The problem, in brief, is whether it refers to:

1. True Christians who subsequently turn away from Christ and are lost.
2. True Christians who backslide but who are still saved.
3. Those who profess to be Christians for a while, who identify themselves with a local church, but who then deliberately turn away from Christ. They were never truly born again, and now they never can be.

No matter which view we hold, there are admitted difficulties. We believe that the third view is the correct one because it is most consistent with the over-all teaching of the Epistle and of the New Testament.

Here in verse 26 apostasy is defined as sinning deliberately after receiving the knowledge of the truth. Like Judas, the person has heard the gospel. He knows the way of salvation; he has even pretended to receive it; but then he deliberately repudiates it.

For such a person, there is no more sacrifice for sins. He has decisively and conclusively rejected the once-for-all sacrifice of Christ. Therefore God has no other way of salvation to offer to him.

The fact that Paul uses "we" in this passage does not necessarily mean that he includes himself. In verse 39 he definitely *excludes* himself and his fellow believers from those who draw back into perdition.

10:27. Nothing remains but a fearful prospect of judgment; there is no hope of escape. It is impossible to renew the apostate to repentance (6:4). He has knowingly and willfully cut himself off from God's grace in

Christ. His fate is a fury of fire which will consume the adversaries. It is pointless to haggle over whether this means literal fire. The language is obviously designed to denote punishment that is dreadfully severe.

Note that God classes apostates as adversaries. This indicates positive opposition to Christ, not a mild neutrality.

10:28. The doom of the lawbreaker in the Old Testament is now introduced to form a backdrop against which to contrast the greater doom of the apostate.

A man who broke Moses' law by becoming an idolater died without mercy when his guilt was proven by the testimony of two or three witnesses (Deuteronomy 17:2-6).

10:29. The apostate will be counted worthy of much sorer judgment because his privilege has been much greater. The enormity of his sin is seen in the three charges that are leveled against him:

1. "He has spurned the Son of God." After professing to be a follower of Jesus, he now brazenly asserts that he wants nothing more to do with Him. He denies any need for Christ as Saviour and positively rejects Him as Lord.

It is said that there is in Japan a crucifix which was used by the government in days of persecution. It was placed on the ground, and everybody had to tread on the face of the Crucified. The non-Christians did not hesitate to tread on His face; the real Christians refused and were killed. The story goes that the face of Jesus was worn down and marred by people treading on it.

2. "He has profaned the blood of the covenant by which he was sanctified." He counts as useless and unholy the blood of Christ which ratified the new covenant. He had been set apart by this blood in a place of external privilege. Through his association with Christian people, he had been sanctified, just as an unbelieving husband is sanctified by his believing wife (1 Corinthians 7:14). But that does not mean that he was saved.

3. "He has outraged the Spirit of grace." The Spirit of God had illuminated him concerning the good news, had convicted him of sin, and had pointed him to Christ as the only Refuge of the soul. But he had insulted the gracious Spirit by utterly despising Him and the salvation He offered.

10:30. Willful repudiation of God's beloved Son is a sin of immense magnitude. God will sit in judgment on all who are guilty of it. He has said, "Vengeance is Mine, I will repay" (see Deuteronomy 32:35). Vengeance in this sense means full justice. When used of God it has no thought of vindictiveness or of getting even. It is simply the meting out of what a person actually deserves. Knowing the character of God, we know that He will do as He has said by repaying the apostate in just measure.

"And again, 'The Lord will judge His people.'" In Deuteronomy 32:36, from which this is quoted, it is translated, "The Lord will vindicate His people." This is true, of course; the Lord will avenge and vindicate those who truly belong to Him. But here in verse 30, the obvious reference is to judgment of evil people.

If it causes difficulty to think of apostates being spoken of as His people, we should remember that they are His by creation and also for a while by profession. He is their Creator though not their Redeemer, and they once professed to be His people, even though they never knew Him personally.

10:31. The abiding lesson for all is this: do not be among those who fall into His hands for judgment, because it is a fearful thing.

Nothing in this passage of Scripture was ever intended to disturb and unsettle the minds of those who truly belong to Christ. The passage was purposely written in its sharp, piercing, searching, challenging style so that all who profess the Name of Christ might be warned as to the terrible consequences of turning away from Him.

VII. *Exhortations   and   Warnings   (10:19—13:17) (continued)*

  F. *Exhortation to endurance (10:32-39)*

    1. *Their past experience should stimulate them*

      a. *Recollection:* But recall the former days

      b. *Illumination:* when, after you were enlightened,

      c. *Persecution:* you endured a hard struggle with sufferings,

        (1) *Individual:* sometimes being publicly exposed to abuse and affliction,

        (2) *Collective:* and sometimes being partners with those so treated.

      d. *Compassion:* For you had compassion on the prisoners,

e. *Confiscation:* and you joyfully accepted the plundering of your property,

f. *Consideration:* since you knew that you yourselves had

   (1) *Better possession:* a better possession
   (2) *Abiding possession:* and an abiding one.

2. *The nearness of the reward should strengthen them*

   a. *The great reward of confidence*: Therefore do not throw away your confidence, which has a great reward.

   b. *The fulfilled promises for endurance:* For you have need of endurance, so that you may do the will of God and receive what is promised.

   c. *The blessed hope of His coming:* "For yet a little while, and the coming one shall come and shall not tarry;

3. *The fear of God's displeasure should deter them*

   a. *The pleasing walk of faith:* but My righteous one shall live by faith,

   b. *The displeasing retreat of apostasy:* and if he shrinks back, My soul has no pleasure in him."

   c. *Apostasy's retribution:* But we are not of those who shrink back and are destroyed,

   d. *Faith's reward:* but of those who have faith and keep their souls.

10:32. In the remaining verses of the chapter, the writer gives three strong reasons why the early Jewish Christians should continue steadfastly in their allegiance to Christ.

    1. Their past experiences should stimulate them.
    2. The nearness of the reward should strengthen them.
    3. The fear of God's displeasure should deter them from going back.

First of all, then, their past experiences should stimulate them. After they professed faith in Christ, they became the targets of bitter persecution: their families disowned them, their friends forsook them, and their foes hounded them. But instead of producing cowardice and fear, these sufferings strengthened them in their faith. Doubtless they felt something of the exhilaration of being counted worthy to suffer dishonor for His Name (Acts 5:41).

10:33. Sometimes their suffering was individual; they were taken out alone and publicly exposed to abuse and affliction. At other times, they suffered with other Christians.

10:34. They were not afraid to visit those who were prisoners for Christ, even though there was always the danger of guilt by association.

When their property was confiscated by the authorities, they accepted it joyfully. They chose to be true to Jesus rather than to keep their material possessions. They knew that they had "an inheritance which is imperishable, undefiled, and unfading" (1 Peter 1:4). It was truly a miracle of divine grace that enabled them to value earthly wealth so lightly.

10:35. The second great consideration is this: the nearness of the reward should strengthen them. Having endured so much in the past, they should not capitulate now. The author says in effect, "Don't miss the harvest of your tears" (F.B. Meyer). They were now nearer the fulfillment of God's promise than ever before. This was no time to turn back.

"Don't throw away your trust now — it carries with it a rich reward in the world to come" (Phillips).

10:36. What they needed was endurance, the determination to remain under the persecutions rather than escape them by denying Christ. Then after having done the will of God, they would receive the promised reward.

10:37. The coming reward is synchronous with the return of the Lord Jesus; hence the quotation from Habakkuk 2:3: "For yet a little while, and the coming one shall come and shall not tarry." Actually the verse in Habakkuk reads; "For still the vision awaits its time; it hastens to the end — it will not lie. If it seem slow, wait for it; it will surely come, it will not delay." Concerning this change Vincent says, "In the Hebrew, the subject of the sentence is the vision of the extermination of the Chaldees. . . . As rendered in the Septuagint either Jehovah or Messiah must be the subject. The passage was referred to Messiah by the later Jewish theologians and is so taken by our writer."

A.J. Pollock comments: "The Old Testament passage and the altered quotation in the New Testament are alike verbally inspired and equally Scripture. The IT in Habakkuk refers to the vision — and deals with the coming of Christ to reign. IT becomes HE in Hebrews and refers to the Rapture." Then he continues in a more general vein: "When an inspired writer quotes from the Old Testament he uses just as much of the passage quoted as suits the purpose of the Divine Mind, though never contradicting it; altering it often in order to convey, not the exact meaning of the Old Testament passage, but the fuller meaning intended to be conveyed by the Holy Spirit in the New Testament. . . . Now no one but God could so treat Scripture. The fact that it is done, and done largely, is another claim to inspiration. God is the Author of the Bible, and He can quote His OWN words, altering and adding to them to suit His purpose. But if any of us quote Scripture, we must do it with careful exactitude. We have no right to alter a jot or tittle. But the Author of the Book can do this. It matters little what pen He uses, whether it be Moses or Isaiah, Peter or Paul, or Matthew or John, it is all His writing."[1]

10:38. A final incentive to steadfast endurance is the fear of God's displeasure. Continuing the quotation from Habakkuk, the author shows that the life that pleases God is the life of faith: "My righteous one shall live by faith." This is the life that values God's promises, that sees the unseen, and that perseveres to the end.

On the other hand the life that displeases God is that

1. *Modernism Versus The Bible* (London: Central Bible Truth Depot, n.d.) p. 19.

of the man who renounces the Messiah and returns to the obsolete sacrifices of the Temple: "if he shrinks back, My soul has no pleasure in him."

10:39. The writer quickly disassociates himself and his fellow believers from those who draw back to destruction. It seems to me that this separates apostates from genuine Christians. Apostates shrink back and are destroyed. True believers have faith and thus preserve their souls from the doom of the renegade.

With this mention of faith, the groundwork is laid for a fuller discussion of the life that pleases God. The memorable eleventh chapter follows quite naturally at this point.

CHAPTER 11

VII. *Exhortations and Warnings* (10:19–13:17) *(continued)*

   G. *The vision and endurance of faith* (11:1-40)

      1. *Faith's amazing capability* (11:1)

         a. *Gives substance to hope:* Now faith is the assurance of things hoped for,

         b. *Sees the invisible:* the conviction of things not seen.

      2. *Faith, the road to renown:* (11:2) For by it the men of old received divine approval.

      3. *Faith and the fact of creation* (11:3)

         a. *The basis of knowledge:* By faith we understand

         b. *The creation of matter:* that the world was created

         c. *The source of matter:* by the word of God,

         d. *The composition of matter:* so that what is seen was made out of things which do not appear.

11:1. This chapter deals with the vision and endurance of faith. It introduces us to men and women of the Old Testament who had 20-20 spiritual vision and who endured tremendous shame and suffering rather than renounce their faith.

Verse 1 is not really a definition of faith; rather it is a description of what faith does for us. It makes things hoped for as real as if we already had them, and it provides unshakable evidence that the unseen, spiritual blessings of Christianity are absolutely certain and real. In other words, it brings the future within the present and makes the invisible seen.

Faith is confidence in the trustworthiness of God. It is the conviction that what God says is true and that what He promises will come to pass.

Faith must have some revelation from God, some promise of God as its foundation. It is not a leap in the dark. It demands the surest evidence in the universe, and finds it in the Word of God. It is not limited to possibilities but invades the realm of the impossible. Someone has said, "Faith begins where possibilities end. If it's possible, then there's no glory for God in it."

> Faith, mighty faith the promise sees,
> And looks to God alone;
> Laughs at impossibilities
> And cries, "It shall be done."

There are difficulties and problems in the life of faith. God tests our faith in the crucible to see if it is genuine (1 Peter 1:7). But "difficulties are food for faith to feed on" (Mueller).

11:2. Because they walked by faith and not by sight, the Old Testament worthies received divine approval. The rest of this chapter is an illustration of how God has borne witness to them.

11:3. Faith provides us with the only factual account of creation. God is the only One who was there; He tells us how it happened. We believe His Word and thus we know. "The conception of God pre-existent to matter and by His fiat calling it into being is beyond the domain of reason or demonstration. It is simply accepted by an act of faith" (McCue).

"By faith we understand." The world says, "Seeing is believing." God says, "Believing is seeing." Jesus said to Martha, "Did I not tell you that if you would believe you would see. . . ." (John 11:40). The Apostle John wrote, "I write this to you who believe . . . that you may know" (1 John 5:13). In spiritual matters faith precedes understanding.

The world was created by the word of God. God spoke and matter came into being. This agrees perfectly with man's discovery that matter is essentially energy. When God spoke, there was a flow of energy in the form of sound waves. These were transformed into matter, and the world sprang into being.

"What is seen was made out of things which do not appear." Energy is invisible; so are atoms, and molecules, and gasses to the naked eye, yet in combination they become visible.

The fact of creation as set forth here in Hebrews 11:3 is unimpeachable. It has never been improved on and never will.

VII. *Exhortations and Warnings* (10:19—13:17) *(continued)*

G. *The vision and endurance of faith* (11:1-40) *(continued)*

    4. *The faith of Abel* (11:4)

        a. *His offering commended:* By faith Abel offered to God a more acceptable sacrifice than Cain,

        b. *His righteousness attested:* through which he received approval as righteous,

        c. *His gifts accepted:* God bearing witness by accepting his gifts;

        d. *His testimony perpetuated:* he died, but through his faith he is still speaking.

    5. *The faith of Enoch* (11:5)

        a. *Miraculous translation:* By faith Enoch was taken up

        b. *Marvelous deliverance:* so that he should not see death;

        c. *Missing patriarch:* and he was not found,

        d. *Mighty power:* because God had taken him.

        e. *Magnificent walk:* Now before he was taken he was attested as having pleased God.

    6. *Essential faith and faith's essentials* (11:6)

        a. *Indispensability:* And without faith it is impossible to please Him.

        b. *Ingredients:* For whoever would draw near to God must believe

            (1) *The existence of God:* that He exists

            (2) *The trustworthiness of God:* and that He rewards those who seek Him.

    7. *The faith of Noah* (11:7)

a. *The basis of faith:* By faith Noah, being warned by God
b. *The realm of faith:* concerning events as yet unseen,
c. *The reverence of faith:* took heed
d. *The response of faith:* and constructed an ark
e. *The quest of faith:* for the saving of his household;
f. *The effect of faith:* by this he condemned the world
g. *The reward of faith:* and became an heir of the righteousness which comes by faith.

11:4. Abel must have had some revelation that sinful man can approach God only on the ground of shed blood. Perhaps he learned this from his parents who were restored to fellowship with God only after He had clothed them with the skins of animals (Genesis 3:21). At any rate, he exhibited faith by approaching God with the blood of a sacrifice. Cain's sacrifice was one of vegetables or fruit and was therefore bloodless. Abel illustrates the truth of salvation by grace through faith. Cain pictures man's futile attempt to save himself by good works.

"It was not the personal excellence of Abel that God looked at in counting him righteous, but the excellence of the sacrifice that he brought and his faith in it" (George Cutting). And so it is with us: we are not justified because of our character or good works, but solely because of the excellence of the sacrifice of Christ and our acceptance of Him.

Abel was killed by Cain because law hates grace. Self-righteous man hates the truth that he cannot save himself and that he must cast himself on the love and mercy of God.

But Abel's testimony is perpetuated: "Through his faith he is still speaking." There is a sense in which faith enables a man's vocal chords to go on functioning long after his body is lying in the grave.

11:5. Sometime during his life Enoch must have received a promise from God that he would go to Heaven without dying. Up to that time everyone had died — sooner or later. There was no record of anyone ever having been translated. But God promised and Enoch believed. It was the most sane, rational thing that Enoch could do; what is more reasonable than that the creature should believe his Creator?

And so it happened! Enoch walked with the invisible God for 300 years (Genesis 5:21-24) and then he walked into eternity. Before his translation he had this testimony — that he pleased God. The life of faith always pleases God; He loves to be trusted.

11:6. Without faith it is impossible to please Him. No amount of good works can compensate for lack of faith. After all is said and done, when a man refuses to believe God, he is calling Him a liar. "He who does not believe God, has made Him a liar" (1 John 5:10), and how can God be pleased by people who call Him a liar?

Faith is the only thing that gives God His proper place, and puts man in his place too. "It glorifies God exceedingly . . . because it proves that we have more confidence in His eyesight than in our own" (C.H. Mackintosh).

Faith not only believes that God exists, but it also trusts Him to reward those who seek Him. There is nothing about God that makes it impossible for men to believe. The difficulty is with the human will.

11:7. Noah's faith was based on God's word that He was going to destroy the world with a flood (Genesis 6:17). There never had been a flood in human experience, in fact, there is some reason to believe that there never had been rainfall up to that time (Genesis 2:5-6). Noah believed God and built an ark, even though he was probably very far from navigable waters. Doubtless he was the butt of many a joke. But Noah's faith was rewarded: his household was saved, the world was condemned by his life and testimony, and he became heir of the righteousness which is received on the basis of faith.

Perhaps many of the early Jewish Christians to whom this letter was written often wondered why, if they were right, they were such a small minority. Noah steps out from the pages of the Old Testament to remind them that in his day only eight people were right and all the rest of the world perished.

VII. *Exhortations and Warnings* (10:19—13:17) *(continued)*

    G. *The vision and endurance of faith* (11:1-40) *(continued)*

        8. *The faith of Abraham* (11:8)

            a. *Unhesitating obedience:* By faith Abraham obeyed

            b. *Unusual call:* when he was called to go

out to a place which he was to receive as an inheritance;

   c. *Unknown destination:* and he went out, not knowing where he was to go.

9. *The faith of Abraham* (11:9-10)

   a. *The fact of his sojourn:* By faith he sojourned

   b. *The land of his sojourn:* in the land of promise,

   c. *The attitude of his sojourn:* as in a foreign land,

   d. *The evidence of his sojourn:* living in tents

   e. *The companions of his sojourn:* with Isaac and Jacob, heirs with him of the same promise.

   f. *The reason for his sojourn*

     (1) *The city:* For he looked forward to the city

     (2) *The foundations:* which has foundations,

     (3) *The Architect:* whose builder

     (4) *The Builder:* and maker is God.

10. *The faith of Sarah* (11:11)

   a. *Miraculous conception:* By faith Sarah herself received power to conceive,

   b. *Natural limitation:* even when she was past the age,

   c. *Unshakable conviction:* since she considered Him faithful who had promised.

11. *The faith of Abraham* (11:12)

a. *Unique paternity:* Therefore from one man,

b. *Faint possibility:* and him as good as dead,

c. *Numerous posterity:* were born descendants

   (1) *Spiritual:* as many as the stars of heaven

   (2) *Physical:* and as the innumerable grains of sand by the seashore.

11:8. Abraham was probably an idolater, living in Ur of the Chaldees, when God appeared to him and told him to move. With the obedience of faith, he left home and country, not knowing his ultimate destination. Doubtless his friends ridiculed him for such folly but his attitude was:

> I go on not knowing —
> I would not if I might,
> I'd rather walk in the dark with God
> Than walk alone in the light;
> I'd rather walk by faith with Him
> Than to walk alone by sight.
>   —Helen Annis Casterline

The walk of faith often gives the impression to others of being imprudent and reckless, but the man who knows God is content to be led blindfolded without knowing the route ahead.

11:9. God had promised the land of Canaan to Abraham. In a very real sense it belonged to him. Yet the only parcel of ground he ever bought in it was a tomb for his dead. He was content to live in a tent, the symbol of pilgrimage, instead of in a fixed abode. For the time being he treated Canaan as if it were a foreign land.

The companions of his pilgrimage were his son and grandson. His godly example left its mark on them also; even though they were heirs of the same promise that the land would be theirs.

11:10. Why did Abraham hold such a light grip on real estate in Canaan? Because he looked for *the* city which has *the* foundations whose Architect and Builder is God. He did not have his heart set on present, material things, but on the eternal. In the ASV there is a definite article before *city* and *foundation* — *the* city and *the* foundation. In the reckoning of faith there is only one city worthy of the name and only one city with sure foundations.

God is the Architect of this heavenly city and He is its Builder as well. It is the model city, without slums, polluted air, polluted water, or any of the other problems that plague our metropolitan centers.

11:11. By faith Sarah was miraculously empowered to conceive when she was about ninety years old. The record clearly states that she was beyond the time of life when she could bear a child. But she knew that God had promised her a baby, and she knew He could not go back on His word. She had shatterproof faith that He would do what He had promised.

11:12. Abraham was about 99 when Isaac was born. Humanly speaking it was just about impossible for him to become a father, yet God had promised a numerous posterity and so it must be.

Through Isaac Abraham became the father of an innumerable earthly family, the Hebrew nation. Through Christ he became father of an innumerable spiritual family, that is, true believers of every subsequent age. The earthly progeny correspond to the numberless grains of sand by the seashore, whereas the heavenly people correspond to the stars of heaven.

VII. *Exhortations and Warnings* (10:19—13:17) *(continued)*

    G. *The vision and endurance of faith* (11:1-40) *(continued)*

        12. *The faith of the patriarchs* (11:13-16)

            a. *Their steadfast conviction:* These all died in faith,

            b. *Their postponed possession:* not having received what was promised,

            c. *Their telescopic vision:* but having seen it

            d. *Their joyful anticipation:* and greeted it from afar,

            e. *Their pilgrim confession:* and having acknowledged that they were strangers and exiles on the earth.

            f. *Their coveted habitation:* For people who speak thus make it clear that they are seeking a homeland.

            g. *Their possible retrogression:* If they had been thinking of that land from which they had gone out, they would have had opportunity to return.

h. *Their celestial destination:* But as it is, they desire a better country, that is, a heavenly one.
i. *Their resulting approbation:* Therefore God is not ashamed to be called their God,
j. *Their eternal compensation:* for He has prepared for them a city.

11:13. The patriarchs died in faith. They did not live to see the fulfillment of the divine promises. For instance, Abraham never saw his numerous progeny. The Hebrew nation never occupied all the land that had been promised to it. The Old Testament saints never saw the fulfillment of the promise of the Messiah. But their telescopic vision brought the promises near, so near that they are pictured as waving at them in joyful anticipation.

They realized that this world was not their final home. They were content to be strangers and exiles here, refusing the urge to nestle or to make themselves comfortable. Their desire was to pass through the world without taking any of its character upon themselves. Their hearts were set on pilgrimage (Psalm 84:5 Knox).

> Oh, bliss to leave behind us
> The fetters of the slave;
> To leave ourselves behind us,
> The graveclothes and the grave!
> To speed, unburdened pilgrims,
> Glad, empty-handed, free;
> To cross the trackless deserts
> And walk upon the sea.
> —Ter Steegen

11:14. Their lives plainly indicated that they were seeking a homeland. Faith implanted a homing instinct in them which was never satisfied by the delights of Canaan. There was always a yen for a better land which they could call home.

11:15. In saying that they were seeking a homeland, the writer wants to make it clear that he is not referring to the land of their birth. If Abraham had desired to return to Mesopotamia, he could have done so, but that was no longer home to him.

11:16. The true explanation is that they were seeking a homeland in Heaven. This is rather remarkable when we remember that most of the promises to the people of Israel had to do with material blessings on this earth. But they had a heavenly hope as well, and this hope enabled them to treat this world as a foreign country.

This spirit of pilgrimage is especially pleasing to God. "He is not ashamed to be called the God of those whose heart and portion are in heaven" (Darby). He has prepared a city for them, and there they find rest and satisfaction and perfect peace.

VII. *Exhortations and Warnings* (10:19—13:17) *(continued)*

   G. *The vision and endurance of faith* (11:1-40) *(continued)*

      13. *The faith of Abraham* (11:17-19)

         a. *The supreme trial:* By faith Abraham, when he was tested,

b. *The summary obedience:* offered up Isaac,

c. *The seeming dilemma*
   (1) *Promise of posterity:* and he who had received the promises
   (2) *Sacrifice of only son:* was ready to offer up his only son,
   (3) *Problem of procreation:* of whom it was said, "Through Isaac shall your descendants be named."

d. *The singular solution*
   (1) *A literal possibility:* He considered that God was able to raise men even from the dead;
   (2) *A figurative reality:* hence, figuratively speaking, he did receive him back.

14. *The faith of Isaac* (11:20)
    a. *The blesser:* By faith Isaac invoked future blessings
    b. *The blest ones:* on Jacob and Esau.

15. *The faith of Jacob* (11:21)
    a. *Dying:* By faith Jacob, when dying,
    b. *Blessing:* blessed each of the sons of Joseph,
    c. *Worshiping:* bowing in worship over the head of his staff.

16. *The faith of Joseph* (11:22)
    a. *Prediction:* By faith Joseph, at the end of his life, made mention of the exodus of the Israelites

   b. *Instruction:* and gave directions concerning his burial.

11:17. We now come to the greatest test of Abraham's faith. God told him to offer up his only son, Isaac, upon the altar. With unhesitating obedience, Abraham set forth to offer to God the dearest treasure of his heart. Was he oblivious of the tremendous dilemma? God had promised him numberless progeny. Isaac was his only son. Abraham was now 117 and Sarah was 108.

11:18. The promise of a great host of descendants was to be fulfilled through Isaac. The dilemma was this: if Abraham killed Isaac, how could the promise ever be fulfilled? Isaac was now 17 and unmarried.

11:19. Abraham knew what God had promised; that was all that mattered. He figured that if God required him to slay his son, God would raise him from the dead in order to fulfill the promise.

Up to this time there had been no recorded case of resurrection from the dead. Human experience had no statistics to offer. In a real sense, Abraham invented the idea of resurrection. His faith in the promise of God drove him to the conclusion that God would have to raise Isaac.

Figuratively speaking, he did receive Isaac back from the dead. He had committed himself to the fact that Isaac must be slain. God credited him with the act. But then the Lord "spared Abraham's heart a pang He would not spare His own" (Grant). He provided a ram to take Isaac's place, and the only begotten son was returned to his father's heart and home.

Before leaving this outstanding example of faith, there are one or two points that should be mentioned. First, God never really intended for Abraham to slay his son. Human sacrifices were never God's will for His people. He tested Abraham's faith and found it to be genuine; then He rescinded His order.

Secondly, Abraham's faith in the promise of a numerous progeny was tested over a period of one hundred years. The patriarch was 75 when the promise of a son was first given. He waited 25 years before Isaac was born. Isaac was 17 when Abraham took him up on Mount Moriah to offer him to God. Isaac was 40 when he married, and was married 20 years before the twins were born. Abraham died when he was 175. At that time his descendants consisted of one son, 75 years of age, and two grandchildren, 15 years of age. Yet during his lifetime, "No distrust made him waver concerning the promise of God, but he grew strong in his faith as he gave glory to God, fully convinced that God was able to do what He had promised" (Romans 4:20-21).

11:20. Perhaps it is difficult for our western minds to understand what was so unusual in the faith of Isaac, Jacob, and Joseph, as recorded in the next three verses. Isaac, for instance, achieved a place in faith's hall of fame because he invoked future blessings on Jacob and Esau. What was remarkable about that?

Before the children were born, the Lord announced to Rebekah that the boys would become the source of two nations and that the elder (Esau) would serve the younger (Jacob). Esau was Isaac's favorite and as the elder son would normally have received the best portion from his father. But Rebekah and Jacob deceived Isaac, whose sight was now poor, into giving the best blessing to Jacob. When the plot was exposed, Isaac trembled violently. But he remembered God's Word that the elder would serve the younger, and in spite of his predilection for Esau, he realized that God's overruling of his natural weakness must stand.

11:21. There were many inglorious chapters in the life of Jacob, but he is honored as a hero of faith nevertheless. His character improved with age and he died in a burst of glory. When he blessed Ephraim and Manasseh, the sons of Joseph, he crossed his hands so that the elder son's blessing fell on Ephraim, the younger. In spite of Joseph's protests, Jacob insisted that the blessing must stand because this was the order which the Lord had specified. Though his physical sight was dim, his spiritual sight was keen.

The closing scene of his life finds him worshiping while leaning on the top of his staff. "This stands in most pleasing contrast with all the previous scenes of his eventful history. It reminds one of a serene evening after a tempestuous day; the sun, which during the day had been hidden from view by clouds, mists, and fogs, sets in majesty and brightness, gilding with his beams the western sky, and holding out the cheering prospect of a bright tomorrow. Thus it is with our aged patriarch. The supplanting, the bargain-making, the cunning, the management, the shifting, the shuffling, the unbelieving selfish fears — all those dark clouds of nature and of earth seem to have passed away, and he comes forth, in

all the calm elevation of faith, to bestow blessing, and
impart dignities, in that holy skillfulness which com-
munion   with   God   can   alone   impart," (C. H.
Mackintosh).

11:22. Joseph's faith also was strong at the close of
his life. He believed God's promise that He would de-
liver the people of Israel out of Egypt. Faith enabled
him to picture the exodus already. It was so sure to him
that he instructed his sons to carry his bones with them
for burial in Canaan. "Thus, while surrounded by
Egypt's pomp and splendor, his heart was not there at
all, but with his people in their future glory and blessing" (William Lincoln).

VII. *Exhortations and Warnings* (10:19–13:17) *(con-
         tinued)*
    G. *The vision and endurance of faith* (11:1-40)
         (continued)
         17. *The faith of Moses' parents* (11:23)
              a. *Seclusion:* By faith Moses, when he was
                  born, was hid for three months by his
                  parents,
              b. *Perception:* because they saw that the
                  child was beautiful;
              c. *Determination:* and they were not afraid
                  of the king's edict.
         18. *The faith of Moses* (11:24-28)
              a. *He refused Egypt's fame*
                  (1) *Maturity:* By faith Moses, when he
                       was grown up,
                  (2) *Loyalty:* refused to be called the son

of Pharaoh's daughter,

b. *He repudiated Egypt's pleasures*
   (1) *Humble association:* choosing rather to share ill-treatment with the people of God
   (2) *Transient gratification:* than to enjoy the fleeting pleasures of sin.

c. *He resigned Egypt's wealth*
   (1) *Reproach esteemed:* He considered abuse suffered for the Christ greater wealth
   (2) *Riches scorned:* than the treasures of Egypt,
   (3) *Reward respected:* for he looked to the reward.

d. *He renounced Egypt's king*
   (1) *The land forsaken:* By faith he left Egypt,
   (2) *The king defied:* not being afraid of the anger of the king;
       (a) *Mastery:* for he endured
       (b) *Motive:* as seeing Him who is invisible.

e. *He rejected Egypt's religion*
   (1) *Passover instituted:* By faith he kept the Passover
   (2) *Blood sprinkled:* and sprinkled the blood,
   (3) *Judgment averted:* so that the Destroyer of the first-born might not touch them.

11:23. It is really the faith of Moses' parents and not of Moses himself that is in view here. As they looked on their baby, they saw he was beautiful — but it was more than physical beauty. They saw that he was a child of destiny, one whom God had marked out for a special work. Their faith that God's purposes would be worked out gave them courage to defy the king's edict and to hide the child for three months.

11:24. By faith Moses himself was able to make several noble renunciations. Though reared in the luxury of Egypt's palace and assured of all the things that men strive for, he learned that "it is not the possession of things but the forsaking of them that brings rest" (J. Gregory Mantle).

First of all, he refused Egypt's fame. He was the adopted son of Pharaoh's daughter and therefore assured of a place in the social elite. But he had been born of better blood — a member of God's chosen earthly people. From this nobility he could not drivel down to Egypt's royalty. In his adult years he made his choice; he would not hide his true nationality to win a few short years of earthly fame. The result? Instead of occupying a line on some obscure cuneiform tablet, he is memorialized in God's eternal Book. Instead of being museumized as an Egyptian mummy, he is famous as a man of God.

11:25. Secondly, he repudiated Egypt's pleasures. Humble association with God's suffering people meant more to him than the transient gratification of his appetites. The privilege of sharing ill-treatment with his own people was greater pleasure to him than dissipation in Pharaoh's court.

11:26. Thirdly, he turned his back on Egypt's wealth. Faith enabled him to see that the fabulous treasure houses of Egypt were worthless in the light of eternity. So he chose to suffer the same kind of reproach as the Messiah would later suffer. Loyalty to God and love for His people were valued by him more than the combined wealth of Pharaoh. He knew that these were the things that would count one minute after he died.

11:27. Then, he also renounced Egypt's king. Emboldened by faith, he made his exit from the land of bondage, careless of the fury of the monarch. It was a clear break from the politics of this world. He feared Pharaoh so little because he feared God so much. He kept his eyes on "the blessed and only Sovereign, the King of kings and Lord of lords, who alone has immortality and dwells in unapproachable light, whom no man has ever seen or can see" (1 Timothy 6:15-16).

11:28. Finally, he rejected Egypt's religion. By instituting the Passover and by sprinkling the blood, he emphatically separated himself from the idolatry of the Egyptians forever. He flung down the gauntlet in defiance of the religious establishment. For him salvation was through the blood of the lamb, not through the waters of the Nile. As a result, the first-born of Israel were spared while the first-born of Egypt were slain by the destroyer.

VII. *Exhortations and Warnings* (10:19—13:17) *(continued)*

G. *The vision and endurance of faith* (11:1-40)
   (continued)
   19. *The faith of Israel at the Red Sea* (11:29)
       a. *Causeway of deliverance:* By faith the
          people crossed the Red Sea as if on dry
          land;
       b. *Cul-de-sac of doom:* but the Egyptians,
          when they attempted to do the same,
          were drowned.
   20. *The faith of Israel at Jericho* (11:30)
       a. *Means:* By faith
       b. *Miracle:* the walls of Jericho fell down
       c. *Method:* after they had been encircled
          for seven days.
   21. *The faith of Rahab* (11:31)
       a. *Conviction:* By faith
       b. *Character:* Rahab the harlot
       c. *Compensation:* did not perish with those
          who were disobedient,
       d. *Cause:* because she had given friendly
          welcome to the spies.

11:29. At first the Red Sea seemed to spell disaster
to the Jewish refugees. With the enemy in hot pursuit,
they seemed to be trapped. But in obedience to God's
Word, they moved forward and the waters parted. "The
Lord drove the sea back by a strong east wind all night,
and made the sea dry land, and the waters were divided"
(Exodus 14:21). When the Egyptians tried to follow,
their chariot wheels became clogged, the waters returned to their usual place, and Pharaoh's hosts were

drowned. Thus the Red Sea became a causeway of deliverance to Israel but a cul-de-sac of doom to the Egyptians.

11:30. The walled city of Jericho was the first military objective in the conquest of Canaan. Reason would claim that such an impregnable fortress could be taken only by superior forces. But faith's methods are different. God uses strategies that appear foolish to men in order to accomplish His purposes. He told the people to encircle the city for seven days. On the seventh day they were to march around it seven times. The priests were to give a loud blast on their trumpets, the people were to shout, and the walls would fall. Military experts would write off the method as ludicrous. But it worked! The weapons of the spiritual warfare are not worldly but have divine power to destroy strongholds (2 Corinthians 10:4).

11:31. We do not know when Rahab the harlot became a worshiper of Jehovah, but it is clear that she did. She abandoned the false religion of Canaan to become a Jewish proselyte. Her faith received a rigorous test when the spies came to her home. Would she be loyal to her country and her fellow countrymen or would she be true to the Lord? She decided to stand on the Lord's side, even if it meant betraying her country. By giving friendly welcome to the spies, she and her family were spared while her disobedient neighbors perished.

VII. *Exhortations and Warnings* (10:19—13:17) *(continued)*

G. *The vision and endurance of faith* (11:1-40)
   (continued)
   22. *Other examples of faith* (11:32-40)
       a. *Great host:* And what more shall I say?
       b. *Gallant heroes:* For time would fail me to tell of Gideon, Barak, Samson, Jephthah, of David and Samuel and the prophets —
       c. *Thrilling triumphs*
          (1) *Military conquests:* who through faith conquered kingdoms,
          (2) *Moral achievements:* enforced justice,
          (3) *Spiritual attainments:* received promises,
          (4) *Physical deliverances*
              (a) *Lions:* stopped the mouths of lions,
              (b) *Fire:* quenched raging fire,
              (c) *Sword:* escaped the edge of the sword,
          (5) *Powerful advancements*
              (a) *Strength:* won strength out of weakness,
              (b) *Might:* became mighty in war,
              (c) *Victory:* put foreign armies to flight.
          (6) *Bodily resurrections:* Women received their dead by resurrection.

11:32. At this point the writer asks a rhetorical

question: "What more shall I say?" He has given an imposing list of men and women who demonstrated faith and endurance in Old Testament times. How many more must he give in order to make his point?

He has not run out of examples, but only out of time. It would take too long to go into details so he will satisfy himself to name a few and catalog some triumphs and testings of faith.

There was Gideon whose army was reduced from 32,000 to 300. First the timid were sent home, then those who thought too much of their own comfort. With a hard core of true disciples, Gideon routed the Midianites.

Then there was Barak. When called to lead Israel to battle against the Canaanites, he agreed only on condition that Deborah would go with him. In spite of this cowardly facet in his character, God saw real trust and lists him among the men of faith.

Samson was another man of obvious weakness. Yet, in spite of that, God detected the faith that enabled him to kill a young lion with his hands, to destroy 30 Philistines in Ashkelon, to slay 1,000 Philistines with the jawbone of an ass, to carry away the gates of Gaza, and finally to pull down the temple of Dagon and slay more Philistines in his death than he had in his life.

Though an illegitimate child, Jephthah rose to be the deliverer of his people from the Ammonites. He illustrates the truth that faith enables a man to rise above his birth and environment and make history for God.

David's faith shines out in his contest with Goliath, in his noble behavior toward Saul, in his capture of Zion, and in countless other episodes. In his psalms, we find his faith crystallized in penitence, praise, and prophecy.

Samuel was the last of Israel's judges and her first prophet. He was God's man for the nation at the time the priesthood failed and the kingdom was introduced. He was one of the greatest leaders in Israel's history.

Add to the list the prophets, a noble band of God's spokesmen, men who were embodied consciences, who would rather die than lie, who would rather go to Heaven with a good conscience than stay on earth with a bad one.

11:33. The writer now turns from naming men of faith to citing their exploits.

They conquered kingdoms. Here our minds turn to Joshua, to the judges (who were really military leaders), to David, and to others.

They enforced justice. Kings like Solomon, Asa, Jehoshaphat, Joash, Hezekiah, and Josiah are remembered for reigns which, though not perfect, were characterized by righteousness.

They received promises. This may mean that God made covenants with them, as in the case of Abraham, Moses, David, and Solomon; or it may mean that they received the fulfillment of the promises, thus demonstrating the truth of God's Word.

They stopped the mouths of lions. Daniel is an outstanding example here (Daniel 6:22), but we should also remember Samson (Judges 14:5-6) and David (1 Samuel 17:34-35).

11:34. They quenched raging fire. The fiery furnace succeeded only in burning the fetters of the three young

Hebrews and setting them free (Daniel 3:25). Thus it proved to be a blessing in disguise.

They escaped the edge of the sword. David escaped Saul's malicious attacks (1 Samuel 19:9-10), Elijah escaped the murderous hatred of Jezebel (1 Kings 19:1-3), and Elisha escaped from the king of Syria (2 Kings 6:15-19).

They won strength out of weakness. Many symbols of weakness are found in the annals of faith. Ehud, for instance, was left-handed; yet he slew the king of Moab (Judges 3:12-22). Jael, a member of "the weaker sex," killed Sisera with a tent-pin (Judges 4:21). Gideon used fragile earthen pitchers in the defeat of the Midianites (Judges 7:20). Samson used the jawbone of an ass to slay 1,000 Philistines (Judges 15:15). They all illustrate the truth that God has chosen the weak things of the world to shame the strong (1 Corinthians 1:27).

They became mighty in war. Faith endowed men with strength beyond what was natural and enabled them to overcome in the face of insurmountable odds.

They put foreign armies to flight. Though often underequipped and greatly outnumbered, the armies of Israel walked off with the victory to the confusion of the foe and the amazement of everyone else.

11:35a. Women received their dead by resurrection. The widow of Zarephath (1 Kings 17:22) and the woman of Shunem (2 Kings 4:34) are cases in point.

VII. *Exhortations and Warnings* (10:19—13:17) *(continued)*

   G. *The vision and endurance of faith* (11:1-40) *(continued)*

22. *Other examples of faith* (11:32-40) *(continued)*

d. *Tremendous trials*

(1) *Executions:* Some were tortured,

(a) *Present loss:* refusing to accept release,

(b) *Future gain:* that they might rise again to a better life.

(2) *Humiliation:*   Others   suffered mocking

(3) *Flagellation:* and scourging,

(4) *Incarceration:* and even chains and imprisonment.

(5) *Lapidation:* They were stoned,

(6) *Mutilation:* they were sawn in two,

(7) *Destruction:* they were killed with the sword;

(8) *Dispossession*

(a) *Destitution:* they went about in skins of sheep and goats, destitute,

(b) *Affliction:* afflicted,

(c) *Persecution:* ill-treated —

(9) *Parenthetical estimation:* of whom the world was not worthy —

(10) *Expulsion:* wandering over deserts and mountains, and in dens and caves of the earth.

e. *Faith witnessed:* And all these, though well attested by their faith,

f. *Fulfillment withheld:* did not receive what was promised,

   g. *God's sovereign provision:* since God had foreseen something better for us,

   h. *Our simultaneous perfection:* that apart from us they should not be made perfect.

35b. But faith has another face. In addition to those who performed dazzling feats, there were those who endured intense suffering. God values the latter as much as the former.

Because of their faith in the Lord, some were subjected to cruel torture. If they would have renounced Jehovah, they would have been released; but to them it was better to die and be raised again to heavenly glory than to continue this life as traitors to God. In the time of the Maccabees, a mother and her seven sons were put to death, one after the other, and in sight of each other, by Antiochus Epiphanes. They refused to accept release.

11:36. Others were mocked and flogged, and were bound in prison. For faithfulness to God, Jeremiah endured all these forms of punishment (Jeremiah 20:1-6; 37:15). Joseph too was imprisoned because he would rather suffer than sin (Genesis 39:20).

11:37. "They were stoned." Jesus reminded the scribes and Pharisees that their ancestors had murdered Zechariah in this way between the sanctuary and the altar (Matthew 23:35).

"They were sawn in two." Tradition says that Manasseh used this method in executing Isaiah.

They "were tempted" (AV). Not all manuscripts include these words in the text. However, the clause probably describes the tremendous pressures that were brought to bear on believers to compromise, to recant, to commit acts of sin, or in any way to deny their Lord.

"They were killed with the sword." Uriah the prophet paid this price for his faithful proclamation of God's message to King Jehoiakim (Jeremiah 26:23); but the expression here refers to mass slaughter such as occurred in the times of the Maccabees.

"They went about in skins of sheep and goats, destitute, afflicted, ill-treated." "They might have rustled in silks and velvets and luxuriated in the palaces of princes had they denied God and believed the world's lie. Instead, they wandered about in sheepskins and goatskins, themselves accounted no better than goats or sheep, nay, they like these reckoned fit only for the slaughter" (Moorhead). They suffered poverty, privation, and persecution.

11:38. The world treated them as if they were not worthy to live. But the Spirit of God bursts forth here with the interjection that actually it was the other way around — the world was not worthy of them.

They wandered over deserts and mountains and in dens and caves of the earth. Dispossessed of homes, separated from families, pursued like animals, expelled from society, they endured heat and cold, distress and hardship, but they would not deny their Lord.

11:39. God has borne witness to the faith of these Old Testament heroes, yet they died before receiving the fulfillment of the promise. They did not live to see the advent of the long-awaited Messiah or to enjoy the blessings that would flow from His ministry.

11:40. God had reserved something better for us. He had arranged that they should not be made perfect apart from us. They never did enjoy a perfect conscience as far as sin was concerned; and they will not enjoy the full perfection of the glorified body in Heaven until we are all caught up to meet the Lord in the air (1 Thessalonians 4:13-18). The spirits of Old Testament saints are already perfect in the presence of the Lord (Hebrews 12:23), but their bodies will not be raised from among the dead until the Lord returns for His people. Then they will enjoy the perfection of resurrection glory.

To put it another way, the Old Testament believers were not as privileged as we are. Yet think of their thrilling triumphs and their tremendous trials! Think of their exploits and their endurance! They lived on the other side of the cross; we live in the full glory of the cross. Yet how do our lives compare with theirs? This is the cogent challenge of Hebrews 11.

CHAPTER 12

VII. *Exhortations and Warnings* (10:19–13:17) *(continued)*

    H. *Renewed exhortation to endurance* (12:1-29)

        1. *The race to be run*

            a. *Witnesses:* Therefore, since we are surrounded by so great a cloud of witnesses,

            b. *Need for unencumbrances*

                (1) *Weights:* let us also lay aside every weight,

                (2) *Sin:* and sin which clings so closely,

            c. *Need for perseverance:* and let us run with perseverance the race that is set before us,

            d. *The foremost Runner:* looking to Jesus

                (1) *Pioneer:* the pioneer

                (2) *Perfecter:* and perfecter of our faith,

                (3) *His motivation:* who for the joy that was set before Him

                (4) *His endurance:* endured the cross,

                (5) *His attitude:* despising the shame,

                (6) *His honor:* and is seated at the right hand of the throne of God.

12:1. We must bear in mind that this Epistle was

written to people who were being persecuted. Because they had forsaken Judaism for Christ, they were facing bitter oppositon. There was a danger that they might interpret their suffering as a sign of God's displeasure. They might become discouraged and give up. Worst of all they might be tempted to return to the Temple and its ceremonies.

They should not think that their sufferings were unique. Many of the witnesses described in chapter 11 suffered severely as a result of their loyalty to the Lord, yet they endured. If they maintained unflinching perseverance with their lesser privileges, how much more should we to whom the better things of Christianity have come.

They surround us as a great cloud of witnesses. This does not mean that they are spectators of what goes on on earth. Rather they witness to us by their lives of faith and endurance and set a high standard for us to duplicate.

This verse invariably raises the question, "Can saints in Heaven see our lives on earth or know what is transpiring?" The only thing we can be sure they know is when a sinner is saved: "Even so, I tell you, there will be more joy in heaven over one sinner who repents than over ninety-nine righteous persons who need no repentance" (Luke 15:7).

The Christian life is a race that requires discipline and endurance. We must strip ourselves of everything that would impede us. Weights are things that may be harmless in themselves and yet hinder progress; they could include material possessions, family ties, the love of comfort, lack of mobility, etc. In the Olympic races, there is no rule against carrying a supply of food and beverage, but the runner would never win the race that way.

We must also lay aside the sin which clings so closely. This may mean sin in any form, but especially the sin of unbelief. We must have complete trust in the promises of God and complete confidence that the life of faith is sure to win.

We must guard against the notion that the race is an easy sprint, that everything in the Christian life is rosy. We must be prepared to press on with perseverance through trials and temptations.

12:2. Throughout the race, we should look away from every other object and keep our eyes riveted on Jesus, the foremost Runner. "One Witness stands out conspicuous above all the rest — the One who perfectly realized the ideal of living by faith. He undauntedly endured the bitter suffering of the cross, and despised the ignominy of it, sustained by a faith that so vividly realized coming joy and glory as to obliterate the consciousness of present pain and shame" (A.B. Bruce).

He is the Pioneer of faith in the sense that He has provided us with the only perfect example of what the life of faith is like.

He is also the Perfecter of faith. He not only began the race but finished it triumphantly. For Him the race course stretched from Heaven to Bethlehem, then on to Gethsemane and Calvary, then out of the tomb and back to Heaven. At no time did He falter or turn back. He kept His eyes fixed on the coming glory when all the redeemed would be gathered with Him eternally. This enabled Him to think nothing of shame and to endure suffering and death. Today He is seated at the right hand of the throne of God.

VII. *Exhortations and Warnings* (10:19—13:17) *(continued)*

   H. *Renewed exhortation to endurance* (12:1-29) *(continued)*

      2. *The fight to be fought* (12:3-4)

         a. *Our undaunted Captain:* Consider Him who endured from sinners such hostility against Himself,

         b. *Our undesirable tendency:* so that you may not grow weary or faint-hearted.

         c. *Our unceasing struggle:* In your struggle against sin

         d. *Our unattained sacrifice:* you have not yet resisted to the point of shedding your blood.

      3. *The discipline to be experienced* (12:5-11)

         a. *Exhortation to sons:* And have you forgotten the exhortation which addresses you as sons? —

            (1) *Despise not:* "My son, do not regard lightly the discipline of the Lord,

            (2) *Faint not:* nor lose courage when you are punished by Him.

         b. *Explanation to sons*

(1) *A token of love:* For the Lord disciplines him whom He loves,

(2) *A proof of sonship:* and chastises every son whom He receives."

(3) *The discipline of endurance:* It is for discipline that you have to endure.

(4) *The significance of discipline:* God is treating you as sons;

    (a) *Question:* for what son is there whom his father does not discipline?

    (b) *Conclusion:* If you are left without discipline, in which all have participated, then you are illegitimate children and not sons.

(5) *Human versus divine discipline*

    (a) *Parental correction:* Besides this, we have had earthly fathers to discipline us

    (b) *Our response to it:* and we respected them.

    (c) *Our greater responsibility to divine discipline:* Shall we not much more be subject to the Father of spirits and live?

    (d) *Defective parental discipline:* For they disciplined us for a short time at their pleasure,

    (e) *Objective divine discipline:* but He disciplines us for our good,

    (f) *Perfective divine discipline:* that

we may share His holiness.

(6) *Evaluation of discipline:*

  (a) *Present pain:* For the moment all discipline seems painful rather than pleasant;

  (b) *Future fruit:* later it yields the peaceful fruit of righteousness to those who have been trained by it.

12:3. The picture now changes from a race to a fight against sin. Our undaunted Captain is the Lord Jesus; no one ever endured such hostility from sinners as He. Whenever we have a tendency to grow weary or fainthearted, we should think of what He went through. Our trials will seem trifling by comparison.

12:4. We are engaged in a ceaseless striving against sin. Yet we have not resisted to the point of shedding our blood, that is, to the point of death. *He did!*

12:5. The Christian view of suffering is now presented. Why do testings, trials, sickness, pain, sorrow, and trouble come into the life of the believer? Are they a sign of God's anger or displeasure? Do they happen by chance? How should we react to them?

These verses teach that these things are part of God's educative process for His children. Although they do not come from God, He overrules them for His glory, for our good, and for the blessing of others.

Nothing happens by chance to the Christian. Tragedies are blessings in disguise, and disappointments are His appointments. God harnesses the adverse circumstances of life to conform us to the image of Christ.

So the early Hebrew believers were exhorted to remember Proverbs 3:11-12, where God addresses them as sons. There He warns them against despising His discipline or losing courage under His reproof. If we rebel or give up, we lose the benefit of His dealings with us and fail to learn His lessons.

12:6. When we read the word chastening, or chastisement, we immediately think of a whipping. But here the word means child training or education. It includes instruction, discipline, correction, and warning. All are designed to cultivate Christian virtues and drive out evil.

The passage in Proverbs distinctly states that God's discipline is a proof of His love, and no son of His escapes chastisement.

12:7. By remaining submissive to the chastening of God, we permit His discipline to mold us into His image. If we try to short-circuit His dealings with us, He may have to teach us over a longer period of time, using more instructive and consequently more difficult methods. There are grades in the school of God, and promotion comes only when we have learned our lessons.

So when testings come to us, we should realize that God is treating us as sons. In any normal father-son relationship, the father trains his son because he loves him and wants the best for him. God loves us too much to let us develop naturally.

12:8. In the spiritual realm, a person who does not experience God's discipline is an illegitimate child, not a true son. After all, the gardener does not prune thistles but he does prune grapevines. As in the natural, so in the spiritual.

12:9. Most of us have experienced discipline from our earthly fathers. We did not interpret this as a sign that they hated us. We realized that they were interested in our welfare, and we respected them.

How much more should we respect the training of the Father of spirits and live! God is the Father of all beings that are spirit or that have a spirit. Man is a spirit dwelling in a human body. By being subject to God we enjoy life in its truest sense.

12:10. The discipline of earthly parents is not perfect. It lasts only for a time, that is, during childhood and youth. If it has not succeeded then, it can do no more. And it is "at their pleasure," in other words, it is according to what they think is right. Sometimes it may not be right.

But God's discipline is always perfect. His love is infinite and His wisdom is infallible. His chastenings are never the result of whim, but always for our profit. His objective is that we might share His holiness. And godliness can never be produced outside God's school.

"The purpose of God's chastening is not punitive but creative. He chastens 'that we may share His holiness.' The phrase 'that we may share' has direction in it, and the direction points toward a purified and beautified life. The fire which is kindled is not a bonfire, blazing heedlessly and unguardedly, and consuming precious things; it is a refiner's fire, and the Refiner sits by it, and He is firmly and patiently and gently bringing holiness out of carelessness and stability out of weakness. God is always creating even when He is using the darker means of grace. He is producing the fruits and flowers of the Spirit. His love is always in quest of lovely things" (J. H. Jowett).

12:11. At the time, all discipline seems painful. But it produces the peaceful fruit of righteousness to those who are exercised by it. That is why we often come across such testimonies as this: "Like all men I love and prefer the sunny uplands of experience, where health, happiness, and success abound, but I have learned far more about God and life and myself in the darkness of fear and failure than I have ever learned in the sunshine. There are such things as the treasures of darkness. The darkness, thank God, passes. But what one learns in the darkness one possesses for ever. 'The trying things,' says Bishop Fenelon, 'which you fancy come between God and you, will prove means of unity with Him, if you bear them humbly. Those things that overwhelm us and upset our pride, do more good than all that which excites and inspirits us' " (Weatherhead). Or the following testimony by C. H. Spurgeon: "I am afraid that all the grace I have got out of my comfortable and easy times and happy hours might almost lie on a penny. But the good that I have received from my sorrows and pains and griefs is altogether incalculable. What do I not owe to the hammer and the anvil, the fire and the file. Affliction is the best bit of furniture in my house."

VII. *Exhortations and Warnings* (10:19—13:17) *(continued)*

    H. *Renewed exhortation to endurance* (12:1-29)

4. *The enthusiasm to be rekindled* (12:12-13)
   a. *Hands:* Therefore lift up your drooping hands
   b. *Knees:* and strengthen your weak knees,
   c. *Feet:* and make straight paths for your feet, so that what is lame may not be put out of joint but rather be healed.
5. *The character to be cultivated* (12:14)
   a. *Peace:* Strive for peace with all men,
   b. *Holiness:* and for the holiness without which no one will see the Lord.
6. *Fifth warning: the sin to shun* (12:15-17)
   a. *Falling short:* See to it that no one fail to obtain the grace of God;
   b. *Bitterness:* that no "root of bitterness" spring up and cause trouble, and by it the many become defiled;
   c. *Immorality:* that no one be immoral
   d. *Irreligiousness:* or irreligious like Esau,
      (1) *Ill-advised decision:* who sold his birthright for a single meal.
      (2) *Irrevocable rejection:* For you know that afterward, when he desired to inherit the blessing, he was rejected,
      (3) *Impossible retraction:* for he found no chance to repent, though he sought it with tears.

12:12. Believers should not buckle under the adverse circumstances of life; their lapse of faith might have an unfavorable influence on others. Drooping hands should be reinvigorated to serve the living Christ. Weak knees should be strengthened for persevering prayer.

12:13. Faltering feet should be guided in straight paths of Christian discipleship. "All who follow the Lord fully, smooth the path of faith to feeble brethren; but those who do not follow fully, roughen the path for others' feet and create spiritual cripples" (George Williams).

"A weary traveler, tired of the road and the buffeting of the tempest, stands dispirited and limp. With shoulders bowed, hands hanging slack, knees bent and shaking, he is ready to give up and sink to the ground. Such can God's pilgrim become, as pictured by our writer.

"But one comes to him confident of mien, with kindly smile and firm voice, and says, 'Cheer up, stand erect, brace your limbs, take heart of grace. You have already come far; throw not away your former toils. A noble home is at the end of the journey. See, yonder is the direct road to it; keep straight on; seek from the great Physician healing for your lameness. . . . Your Forerunner went this same hard road to the palace of God; others before you have won through; others are on the way; you are not alone; only press on! and you too shall reach the goal and win the prize.'

"Happy is he who knows 'how to sustain with words him that is weary' (Isaiah 50:4). Happy is he who accepts exhortation (Hebrews 13:22). And thrice happy is he whose faith is simple and strong, so that he finds no occasion of stumbling in the Lord when His discipline is severe" (G. H. Lang).

12:14. Christians should strive for peaceable relations with all men and at all times. But this exhortation is especially needful when persecution is prevalent, when some are defecting from the faith, and when nerves are frayed. At such times it is all too easy to vent one's frustration and fears on those who are nearest and dearest.

We should also strive for the holiness without which no one will see the Lord. What is the holiness referred to here? To answer the question we should remind ourselves that holiness is used in at least three different ways in the New Testament.

First of all, the believer becomes *positionally* holy at the time of his conversion; he is set apart to God from the world (1 Corinthians 1:2; 6:11). By virtue of his union with Christ, he is sanctified forever. This is what Martin Luther meant when he said, "My holiness is in Heaven." Christ is our holiness, that is, as far as our standing before God is concerned.

Then there is a *practical* sanctification, (1 Thessalonians 4:3; 5:23). This is what we should be day by day. We should separate ourselves from every form of evil. This holiness should be progressive, that is, we should be growing more and more like the Lord Jesus all the time.

Finally there is *complete* or *perfect* sanctification. This takes place when a believer goes to Heaven. Then he is forever free from sin. His old nature is removed, and his state perfectly corresponds to his standing.

Now which holiness are we to strive after? Obviously it is practical sanctification that is in view. We do not strive after positional sanctification; it is ours automatically when we are born again. And we do not strive after the perfect sanctification that will be ours when we see His face. But practical or progressive sanctification is something that involves our obedience and co-operation; we must cultivate this holiness continually.

"The exhortation is to the born-again Jews who had left the Temple, to live such consistent saintly lives, and to cling so tenaciously to their new-found faith, that the unsaved Jews who had also left the Temple and had outwardly embraced the New Testament truth, would be encouraged to go on to faith in Messiah as High Priest, instead of returning to the abrogated sacrifices of the Levitical system. These truly born-again Jews are warned that a limping Christian life would cause these unsaved Jews to be turned out of the way" (Wuest).

But a difficulty remains! Is it true that we cannot see God without practical sanctification? Yes, there is a sense in which this is true; but let us understand that this does not mean that we earn the right to see God by living holy lives. Jesus Christ is our only title to Heaven. What this verse means is that there must be practical holiness as a proof of new life within. If a person is not growing more holy, he is not saved. When the Holy Spirit indwells a person, He manifests His presence by a separated life. It is a matter of cause and effect; if Christ has been received, the rivers of living water will flow.

12:15. The next two verses seem to present four distinct sins to avoid. But there is a strong suggestion in the context that this is another warning against the single sin of apostasy and that these four sins are all related to it.

First of all, apostasy is a failure to obtain the grace of God. The person looks like a Christian, talks like a Christian, professes to be a Christian, but he has never been born again. He has come so near to the Saviour but has never received Him; so near and yet so far.

Apostasy is a root of bitterness. The person turns sour against the Lord and repudiates the Christian faith. His defection is contagious. Others are defiled by his complaints, his doubts, and his denials.

12:16. Apostasy is closely linked with immorality. A professing Christian may fall into gross moral sin. Instead of acknowledging his guilt, he blames the Lord and falls away. Apostasy and sexual sin are connected in 2 Peter 2:10,14,18; Jude 8,16,18.

Finally, apostasy is a form of irreligion, illustrated by Esau. He had no real appreciation for the birthright; he willingly bartered it for the momentary gratification of his appetite.

12:17. Later Esau was remorseful at the loss of the elder son's double portion, but it was too late. His father could not reverse the blessing.

So it is with the apostate. He has no real regard for spiritual values. He willingly renounces Christ in order to escape reproach, suffering, or martyrdom. He cannot be renewed unto repentance. There may be remorse but no godly repentance.

VII. *Exhortations and Warnings* (10:19–13:17) *(continued)*

H. *Renewed exhortation to endure* (12:1-29)
    (continued)
    7. *The privileges to be valued* (12:18-24)
        a. *Not the terrors of Sinai*
            (1) *The mount:* For you have not
                come to what may be touched,
            (2) *The fire:* a blazing fire,
            (3) *The obscurity:* and darkness,
            (4) *The gloom:* and gloom,
            (5) *The tempest:* and a tempest,
            (6) *The trumpet:* and the sound of a
                trumpet,
            (7) *The voice:* and a voice
                (a) *Requested   suspension:*
                    whose words made the hear-
                    ers entreat that no further
                    messages be spoken to
                    them.
                (b) *Fatal injunction:* For they
                    could not endure the order
                    that was given, "If even a
                    beast touches the mountain,
                    it shall be stoned."
            (8) *The terror:* Indeed, so terrifying
                was the sight that Moses said, "I
                tremble with fear."

12:18. Those who are tempted to return to the law
should remember the terrifying circumstances that
attended the giving of the law and should draw spiritual

lessons from it. The scene was Mount Sinai, a literal, tangible mountain that was all on fire. It was enveloped in a pall or veil that made everything seem indistinct, obscure, and nebulous. A violent storm raged around it.

12:19. In addition to these natural disorders, there were terrible supernatural phenomena. A trumpet blasted away, and a voice thundered out so ominously that the people pled for it to stop.

12:20. They were completely unnerved by the divine edict that if even an animal touched the mountain, it should be stoned to death. They knew that if it meant death to a dumb, uncomprehending animal, how much more surely would it mean death to them who understood the warning.

12:21. The entire scene was so frightening and forbidding that Moses himself was shaking.

All this speaks eloquently of the nature and ministry of the law. It is a revelation of God's righteous requirements and of His wrath against sin. The purpose of the law was not to provide the knowledge of salvation but to produce the knowledge of sin. It speaks of distance between God and man because of sin. It is a ministry of condemnation, darkness, and gloom.

VII. *Exhortations and Warnings* (10:19–13:17) *(continued)*

    H. *Renewed exhortation to endure* (12:1-29) *(continued)*

        7. *The privileges to be valued* (12:18-24) *(continued)*

            b. *But the welcome of grace*

(1) *Mount Zion:* But you have come to Mount Zion

(2) *Heavenly Jerusalem:* and to the city of the living God, the heavenly Jerusalem,

(3) *Angelic hosts:* and to innumerable angels in festal gathering,

(4) *The Church:* and to the assembly of the first-born who are enrolled in heaven,

(5) *God, the Judge:* and to a judge who is God of all,

(6) *Old Testament saints:* and to the spirits of just men made perfect,

(7) *The Lord Jesus:* and to Jesus, the mediator of a new covenant,

(8) *The sprinkled blood:* and to the sprinkled blood that speaks more graciously than the blood of Abel.

12:22. Believers have not come to the forbidding terrors of Sinai but to the welcome of grace.

> The burning mount and the mystic veil,
> With our terrors and guilt are gone;
> Our conscience has peace that can never fail,
> 'Tis the Lamb on high on the throne.
> —James G. Deck

Now every blood-bought child of God can say,

> The terrors of law and of God,
> With me can have nothing to do;

> My Saviour's obedience and blood
> Hide all my transgressions from view.
> —A. M. Toplady

"We *have* already arrived in principle where in full reality we shall be forever. The future is already the present. In today we possess tomorrow. On earth we own Heaven."

We do not come to a tangible mountain on earth. Our privilege is to enter the sanctuary in Heaven. By faith, we approach God in confession, praise, and prayer. We are not limited to one day of the year, but may enter the holiest at any time with the knowledge that we are always welcome. God no longer says, "Stay at a distance"; He says, "Come near with confidence."

Law has its Sinai but faith has its Zion. This heavenly mount symbolizes the combined blessings of grace — all that is ours through the redeeming work of Christ Jesus.

Law has its earthly Jerusalem but faith has its capital above. The city of the living God is in Heaven, the city which has the foundations whose Architect and Builder is God.

As we enter the presence of God, we are surrounded by an august gathering. First of all, there are myriads of angels who though untainted by sin cannot join with us in song because they do not know "the joy that our salvation brings."

12:23. Then we are with the assembly of the first-born ones who are enrolled in Heaven. These are members of the Church, the Body and Bride of Christ, who have died since Pentecost and are now consciously enjoying the Lord's presence. They await the day when their bodies will be raised from the grave in glorified form and reunited with their spirits.

By faith we see a Judge who is God of all. No longer does darkness and gloom hide Him; to faith's vision His glory is transcendent.

The Old Testament saints are there, the spirits of just men made perfect. Justified by faith, they stand in spotless purity because the value of Christ's work has been imputed to their account. They too await the time when the grave will yield up its ancient charges and they will receive glorified bodies.

12:24. The Lord Jesus is there, the Mediator of a new covenant.

There is a difference between Moses as mediator of the old covenant and Jesus as Mediator of the new. Moses served as a mediator simply by receiving the law from God and delivering it to the people of Israel. He was the go-between, or the people's representative, offering the sacrifices by which the covenant was ratified.

Christ is Mediator of the new covenant in a far higher sense. Before God could righteously make this covenant, the Lord Jesus had to die. He had to seal the covenant with His own blood and give Himself a ransom for all (1 Timothy 2:6).

He secured the blessings of the new covenant for His people by His death. He insures these blessings for them by His endless life. And He preserves His people to enjoy the blessings in a hostile world by His present ministry at God's right hand. All this is included in His mediatorial work.

Bearing the scars of Calvary, the Lord Jesus is exalted at God's right hand, a Prince and a Saviour.

> We love to look up and behold Him there,
> The Lamb for His chosen slain;
> And soon shall His saints all His glories share,
> With their Head and their Lord shall reign.
> —James G. Deck

Finally, there is the sprinkled blood that speaks more graciously than the blood of Abel. When Christ ascended, He presented to God all the value of the blood He shed at the cross. There is no suggestion that He literally carried His blood into Heaven, but the merits of His blood have been made known in the Sanctuary.

> His precious blood is sprinkled there,
> Before and on the throne;
> And His own wounds in Heaven declare
> The work that saves is done.
> —James G. Deck

His precious blood is contrasted with the blood of Abel. Whether we understand the latter as meaning the blood of Abel's sacrifice or Abel's own blood which was shed by Cain, it is still true that Christ's blood speaks more graciously. The blood of Abel's sacrifice said, "Covered temporarily"; Christ's blood says, "Forgiven forever." Abel's own blood cried, "Vengeance"; Christ's blood cries, "Mercy, pardon, and peace."

VII. *Exhortations and Warnings* (10:19—13:17) *(continued)*

   H. *Renewed exhortation to endure* (12:1-29) *(continued)*

      8. *The God to be heeded* (12:25-29): See that you do not refuse Him who is speaking.

         a. *The inescapable earthly warning:* For if they did not escape when they refused Him who warned them on earth,

b. *The less-escapable heavenly warning:* much less shall we escape if we reject Him who warns from heaven.

c. *The earth-shaking voice:* His voice then shook the earth;

d. *The heaven-shaking voice:* but now He has promised, "Yet once more I will shake not only the earth but also the heaven."

e. *Shakable things removed:* This phrase, "Yet once more," indicates the removal of what is shaken, as of what has been made,

f. *Unshakable things remaining:* in order that what cannot be shaken may remain.

g. *Our unshakable kingdom:* Therefore let us be grateful for receiving a kingdom that cannot be shaken,

h. *Our appropriate worship:* and thus let us offer to God acceptable worship, with reverence and awe;

i. *Our awesome God:* for our God is a consuming fire.

12:25. These closing verses of the chapter contrast God's revelation at Sinai with His revelation in and through Christ. The incomparable privileges and glories of the Christian faith are not to be treated lightly. God is speaking, inviting, wooing. To refuse Him is to perish.

Those who disobeyed the voice of God as it was

heard in the law were punished accordingly. When privilege is greater, responsibility is also greater. In Christ, God has given His best and final revelation. Those who reject His voice as it now speaks from Heaven in the gospel are more responsible than those who broke the law. Escape is impossible.

12:26. At Sinai God's voice caused an earthquake. But when He speaks in the future His voice will also produce a heavenquake. This was, in substance, predicted by the Prophet Haggai (2:6): "Yet once more I will shake not only the earth but the heaven."

This shaking will take place during the period from the rapture to the end of Christ's kingdom. Prior to Christ's coming to reign there will be violent convulsions of nature both on earth and in the heavens. Planets will be moved out of orbit causing raging tides and roaring seas. Then at the close of Christ's millennial reign, the earth, the stellar heavens, and the atmospheric heavens will be destroyed by fervent heat (2 Peter 3:10-12).

12:27. When God said, "Yet once more," He anticipated a complete and final removal of the heavens and the earth. This event will explode the myth that what we can see and touch and handle is real and that unseen things are unreal. When God ends the sifting and shaking process, only that which is real will remain.

12:28. Those who were occupied with the tangible, visible ritualism of Judaism were clinging to things that could be shaken. True believers have a kingdom which can never be shaken. This should inspire the most fervent worship and adoration. We should unceasingly praise Him with reverence and awe.

12:29. God is a consuming fire to all who refuse to listen to Him. But even to His own, His holiness and righteousness are so great that they should produce profoundest homage and respect.

CHAPTER 13

VII. *Exhortations and Warnings* (10:19–13:17)
(*continued*)

    I. *Graces to develop* (13:1-6)

      1. *Love of the brethren:* Let brotherly love continue.

      2. *Hospitality for strangers:* Do not neglect to show hospitality to strangers, for thereby some have entertained angels unawares.

      3. *Care for imprisoned believers:* Remember those who are in prison, as though in prison with them;

      4. *Sympathy for suffering saints:* and those who are ill-treated, since you also are in the body.

      5. *Purity in marriage*

        a. *Principle:* Let marriage be held in honor among all,

        b. *Practice:* and let the marriage bed be undefiled;

        c. *Reason:* for God will judge the immoral and adulterous.

      6. *Contentment*

        a. *The sin to avoid:* Keep your life free from love of money,

        b. *The attitude to cultivate:* and be content

with what you have;

    c. *The promise to claim:* for He has said, "I will never fail you nor forsake you."

    d. *The confidence to confess:* Hence we can confidently say, "The Lord is my helper, I will not be afraid; what can man do to me?"

13:1. The practical section of the Epistle continues with six exhortations concerning graces that should be developed. First is love of the brethren. There should be a sense of family relationship toward all true Christians and a recognition of this kinship by loving words and acts (1 John 3:18).

13:2. The readers are urged to show hospitality to strangers. This might refer primarily to believers who were fleeing from persecution and were hard-pressed to find food and lodging; to entertain them was to expose the host and hostess to danger. The verse may also be understood as a general encouragement to show hospitality to any believers who need it.

There is always the thrilling possibility that in doing this we may entertain angels unawares. This of course looks back to Abraham's experience with three men who were actually angelic beings (Genesis 18:1-15). Even if we never have real angels in our homes, we may have men and women whose very presence is a benediction and whose godly influence on our family may have results that reach on into eternity.

13:3. The third exhortation concerns care for imprisoned believers. This almost certainly means those who were jailed because of their testimony for Christ. They would need food, warm clothing, reading matter, and encouragement. The temptation would be for other believers to shield themselves from association with prisoners and thus from the danger of guilt by association. They should remember that in visiting the prisoner, they were visiting Christ.

Compassion should also be shown for the ill-treated; again this doubtless means persecuted Christians. The readers should resist any tendency to shield themselves from the danger that such compassion might involve. For ourselves, we can broaden the application of the verse to include sympathy for all suffering saints. We should remember that we too are in the body and therefore subject to similar afflictions.

13:4. Marriage should be held in honor by all. We should remember that it was instituted by God before sin entered the world and that it is His holy will for mankind. To treat it as unclean, as ascetics do, or even to make jests and puns about it, as Christians sometimes do, are alike forbidden.

Those who are married should be faithful to their vows and thus keep the marriage bed undefiled. In spite of modern man's smug laxness in this area, the fact remains that any sexual relations outside the bounds of marriage are sin. Many psychologists notwithstanding, adultery is not sickness; it is sin. And it is a sin which God will inevitably judge. No form of immorality will escape. He judges it in this life — through bodily ailments, through broken families, through mental and nervous afflictions, through personality deformities. Unless it is pardoned through the blood of Christ, He will judge it in eternal fire.

Bishop Latimer reminded the immoral King Henry VIII of this in a way that was as convicting as it was courageous. He presented the king with a finely wrapped Bible. On the wrapping was inscribed the words, "Fornicators and adulterers God will judge."

13:5. The sixth virtue to cultivate is contentment. Remember that the adherents of Judaism were continually saying, "We have the Tabernacle. We have the priesthood. We have the offerings. We have the beautiful ritual. What do you have?" Here the writer quietly says to the Christians: "Keep your life free from love of money, and be content with what you have." I should say so! What the Christian has is so infinitely greater than the best of Judaism — why shouldn't he be content? He has Christ; that is enough.

The love of silver can be a tremendous weight to the believer. Just as a small silver coin held before the eye comes between it and the sun, so covetousness breaks fellowship with God and hinders spiritual progress.

The greatest riches a person can have lie in possessing Him who promises, "I will never fail you nor forsake you."

13:6. The words of Psalm 118:6 are the confident confession of the one who has Christ: "With the Lord on my side I do not fear. What can man do to me?" The fact is that in Christ we have perfect security, perfect protection, perfect peace.

VII. *Exhortations and Warnings* (10:19—13:17) *(continued)*
   J. *Past leaders to respect* (13:7-8)

1. *Remember their leadership:* Remember your leaders,
2. *Recall their instruction:* those who spoke to you the word of God;
3. *Consider their goal:* consider the outcome of their life,
4. *Imitate their faith:* and imitate their faith. Jesus Christ is the same yesterday and today and for ever.

K. *False teachings to avoid* (13:9): Do not be led away by diverse and strange teachings;
   1. *A fact attested:* for it is well that the heart be strengthened by grace, not by foods,
   2. *A fallacy exposed:* which have not benefited their adherents.

L. *An altar to frequent* (13:10-16)
   1. *Possession:* We have an altar
   2. *Exclusion:* from which those who serve the tent have no right to eat.
   3. *Separation*
      a. *Where the sacrifices were burned:* For the bodies of those animals whose blood is brought into the sanctuary by the high priest as a sacrifice for sin are burned outside the camp.
      b. *Where Jesus suffered:* So Jesus also suffered outside the gate in order to sanctify the people through His own blood.
      c. *Where we should go:* Therefore let us go forth to Him outside the camp, bearing abuse for Him.

4. *Destination:* For here we have no lasting city, but we seek the city which is to come.
5. *Adoration:* Through Him then let us continually offer up a sacrifice of praise to God, that is, the fruit of our lips that acknowledge His name.
6. *Benefaction:* Do not neglect to do good and to share what you have, for such sacrifices are pleasing to God.

M. *Present leaders to obey* (13:17)
1. *Our duty to them:* Obey your leaders and submit to them;
2. *Their care for us:* for they are keeping watch over your souls,
3. *Their solemn responsibility:* as men who will have to give account.
4. *Their sincere desire:* Let them do this joyfully, and not sadly,
5. *Our disadvantage:* for that would be of no advantage to you.

13:7. The readers are instructed to remember their past leaders, the early Christian teachers who spoke God's Word to them. What was the outcome of their lives? They had not turned back to the Levitical system but had maintained their confession steadfast to the end. Perhaps some of them were martyred for Christ's sake. Theirs is the faith to imitate, the faith that clings to Christ and to the Christian faith, and that brings God into every move in life. We are not all called to the same forms of service, but we are all called to a life of faith.

13:8. The connection of this verse with the preceding one is not clear. Perhaps the simplest way to understand it is as a summary of the teaching, the goal, and the faith of these leaders. The gist of their teaching was this: "Jesus Christ is the same yesterday and today and for ever." The goal of their lives was this: "Jesus Christ, the same yesterday and today and for ever." The foundation of their faith was this: "Jesus is the Messiah, the same yesterday and today and for ever."

13:9. Next follows a warning against the false teachings of legalism. The Judaizers insisted that holiness was connected with externals, such as ceremonial worship and clean foods, for example. The truth is that holiness is produced by grace, not by law. Legislation concerning clean and unclean foods was designed to produce ritual cleanness. But this is not the same thing as inward holiness. A man might be ceremonially clean and yet be filled with hatred and hypocrisy. Only God's grace can inspire and empower believers to live holy lives. Love for the Saviour who died on account of our sins motivates us "to live sober, upright, and godly lives in this world" (Titus 2:12). After all, endless rules concerning foods and drinks have not benefited their adherents.

13:10. Let us not miss the triumph of the words, "We have an altar." They are the Christian's confident answer to the repeated taunts of the Judaizers. Our altar is Christ, and therefore it includes all the blessings that are found in Him. Those who are connected with the Levitical system have no right to partake of the better things of Christianity. They must first repent of their sins and believe in Jesus Christ as only Lord and Saviour.

13:11. Under the sacrificial system, certain animals were slain and their blood was brought into the most holy place by the high priest as a sacrifice for sin. The bodies of those animals were carried to a place away from the tabernacle environs and burned. "Outside the camp" means outside the outer fence that enclosed the tabernacle court.

13:12. The animals burned outside the camp were a type; the Lord Jesus was the antitype. He was crucified outside the city walls of Jerusalem. It was outside the camp of organized Judaism that He sanctified the people through His blood.

13:13. The application for the early readers of the Epistle was this: they should make a clean break with Judaism. Once for all they should turn their backs on the temple sacrifices and appropriate the finished work of Christ as their sufficient sacrifice.

The application for us is similar: the camp today is the entire religious system that teaches salvation by works, by character, by ritual, or by ordinances. It is the modern church system with its humanly ordained priesthood, its material aids to worship, and its ceremonial trappings. It is corrupt Christendom, a church without Christ. The Lord Jesus is outside and we should go forth to Him, bearing His reproach.

13:14. Jerusalem was dear to the hearts of those who served at the Temple. It was the geographical center of their "camp." The Christian has no such city on earth; his heart is set on the heavenly city, the new Jerusalem, where the Lamb is all the glory.

13:15. In the New Testament all believers are priests. They are holy priests, going into the sanctuary of God to worship (1 Peter 2:5), and they are royal priests going out into the world to witness (1 Peter 2:9). There are at least three sacrifices which a believer-priest offers. First, there is the sacrifice of his person (Romans 12:1). Then here in verse 15 is the second, namely the sacrifice of his praise. It is offered to God through the Lord Jesus. All our praise and prayer passes through the Lord Jesus before it reaches God the Father; our great High Priest removes all impurities and imperfections and adds His own virtue to it.

> To all our prayers and praises
> Christ adds His sweet perfume;
> And love the censer raises
> These odors to consume.
> —Mary B. Peters

The sacrifice of praise is the fruit of lips that acknowledge His Name. The only worship that God receives is that which flows from redeemed lips.

13:16. The third sacrifice is the offering of our possessions. We are to use our material resources in doing good, and in sharing with those who are in need. This sacrificial living is pleasing to God. It is the opposite of accumulating for self.

> The race of God's anointed priests
> Shall never pass away;
> Before His glorious Face they stand,
> And serve Him night and day.
> Though reason raves, and unbelief
> Flows on a mighty flood,
> There are, and shall be, till the end,

The hidden priests of God.
His chosen souls, their earthly dross
Consumed in sacred fire,
To God's own heart their hearts ascend
In flame of deep desire;
The incense of their worship fills
His Temple's holiest place;
Their song with wonder fills the Heavens,
The glad new song of grace.
                    —Gerhardt Ter Steegen

13:17. In verses 7 and 8, the readers were instructed to remember their past leaders. Now they are taught to obey their present leaders. This probably refers primarily to the elders in the local church. These men act as representatives of God in the assembly. Authority has been given to them, and believers should submit to this authority. As undershepherds, the elders keep watch over the souls of the flock. They will have to give account to God in a coming day. They will do it either joyfully or sadly, depending on the spiritual progress of their charges. If they have to do it sadly, that will mean loss of reward for the saints concerned. So it is to everyone's benefit to respect the lines of authority which God has laid down.

VIII. *Conclusion* (13:18-25)

    A. *The writer's need for prayer* (13:18-19): Pray for us,

        1. *The basis of the appeal:* for we are sure that we have a clear conscience, desiring to act honorably in all things.

        2. *The nature of the appeal:* I urge you the

more earnestly to do this in order that I may be restored to you the sooner.

B. *The writer's parting prayer* (13:20-21)

   1. *To whom it is addressed:* Now may the God of peace

   2. *What He has done:* who brought again from the dead our Lord Jesus, the great shepherd of the sheep, by the blood of the eternal covenant,

   3. *What He is asked to do*

      a. *Perfect equipment:* equip you with everything good

      b. *Perfect obedience:* that you may do His will,

      c. *Perfect inworking:* working in you that which is pleasing in His sight,

      d. *Perfect Executor:* through Jesus Christ;

   4. *What He deserves:* to whom be glory for ever and ever. Amen.

C. *Closing greetings* (13:22-25)

   1. *Exhortation:* I appeal to you, brethren, bear with my word of exhortation, for I have written to you briefly.

   2. *Information:* You should understand that our brother Timothy has been released, with whom I shall see you if he comes soon.

   3. *Salutation:* Greet all your leaders and all the saints. Those who come from Italy send you greetings.

   4. *Benediction:* Grace be with all of you. Amen.

13:18. As the writer comes to the close of his letter, he adds a personal appeal for prayer. The rest of the verse suggests that he may have been under attack from critics. We can guess who the critics were — those who were coercing people to return to the worship of the Old Covenant. He protests that in spite of any charges that were being brought against him, his conscience was clear and his desire was pure.

13:19. An added reason for prayer was that he might be restored to them the sooner. Perhaps this refers to release from prison. We can do no more than speculate on this point.

13:20. Then he adds one of the most beautiful benedictions of the Bible — one that takes its place with Numbers 6:24-26; 2 Corinthians 13:14; and Jude 24-25. It is addressed to the God of peace. As has been mentioned, Old Testament saints never had perfect peace of conscience. But under the New Covenant, we have peace with God (Romans 5:1) and the peace of God (Philippians 4:7). The verse goes on to explain that this peace is the fruit of Christ's work. God raised the Lord Jesus from the dead as a sign that His work on the cross settled the sin question once for all.

Christ, as the good Shepherd, gave His life for the sheep (John 10:11). As the great Shepherd, He rose from the dead, having accomplished redemption (here). As the chief Shepherd, He is coming again to reward His servants (1 Peter 5:4). We see Him as the good Shepherd in Psalm 22, as the great Shepherd in Psalm 23, and as the chief Shepherd in Psalm 24.

He was brought again from the dead in accordance

with the eternal covenant. "The New Testament is called the eternal one, in contrast to the First Testament which was of a transitory nature. It was within the sphere of the eternal covenant that Messiah, having died for sinful man, was raised up from among those who are dead. He could not be a high priest after the order of Melchizedek if He was not raised from the dead. Sinful man needs a living Priest to give life to the believing sinner, not a dead priest merely to pay for his sins. Thus, it was provided within the New Testament that the priest who offered Himself for sacrifice would be raised from the dead" (Wuest).

13:21. The prayer is that the saints might be equipped with everything good to do God's will. Notice here that there is a curious mingling of the divine and the human. God equips us with everything good. God works in us that which is well pleasing in His sight. He does it through Jesus Christ. Then we do His will. In other words, He places the desire in us; He gives us the power to do it; then we do it; and He rewards us.

The prayer ends with the acknowledgment that Jesus Christ is worthy of glory forever and ever.

> Worthy of homage and of praise,
> Worthy by all to be adored;
> Exhaustless theme of heavenly lays,
> Thou, Thou art worthy, Jesus Lord.
> —Frances Ridley Havergal

13:22. The writer now urges his readers to heed the exhortation of his letter, that is, to abandon ritualistic religion and cleave to Christ with true purpose of heart.

He speaks of his Epistle as a brief one, and it is,

considering how much more he could have said about the Levitical system and how it finds its fulfillment in Christ.

13:23. The mention of Timothy's release here confirms many in their view that Paul wrote the letter. There is the added touch that the writer plans to travel with Timothy, another possible sign pointing to Paul. But we cannot be sure, so it is best to leave the question open.

13:24. Greetings are sent to all the Christian leaders and to all the saints. We should not overlook the many touches of Christian courtesy in the Epistles, and we should imitate them in our day.

Some Italian Christians were with the writer, and they too wanted to send their greetings. This does not necessarily mean that the letter was written from Italy.

13:25. It is especially fitting that this Epistle of the New Covenant should end on a grace note: "Grace be with all of you. Amen." The New Covenant is an unconditional covenant of free grace, telling out God's unbounded favor for unworthy sinners through the sacrificial work of the Lord Jesus Christ.

THE MESSAGE OF THE EPISTLE FOR TODAY

Does the Epistle to the Hebrews have a message for us in the twentieth century?

Although Judaism is not the dominating religion today that it was in the early days of the Church, yet the spirit of Judaism has permeated Christendom. In his well-known booklet, *Rightly Dividing the Word of Truth,* Dr. C. I. Scofield wrote: "It may be safely said that the *Judaising of the Church* has done more to hinder her progress, pervert her mission, and destroy her spirituality, than all other causes combined. Instead of pursuing her appointed path of separation from the world and following the Lord in her heavenly calling, she has used Jewish Scriptures to justify herself in lowering her purpose to the civilization of the world, the acquisition of wealth, the use of an imposing ritual, the erection of magnificent churches . . . and the division of an equal brotherhood into 'clergy' and 'laity.' "

The letter calls on us to separate ourselves from all religious systems in which Christ is not honored as the only Lord and Saviour and in which His work is not recognized as the once-for-all offering for sin.

The Epistle teaches us that the types and shadows of the Old Testament system found their fulfillment in our Lord. He is our great High Priest. He is our Sacrifice. He is our Altar. He serves in the heavenly sanctuary and His priesthood will never end.

It teaches that all believers are priests, and that they have instant access into the presence of God by faith at any time. They offer the sacrifices of their person, their praise, and their possessions.

In *The New Order of Priesthood,* David Baron writes: "To adopt the model of the Levitical priesthood in the Christian Church, which ritualism endeavors to do, is nothing else but an attempt, with unholy hands, to sew together again the veil which the blessed, reconciled God had Himself rent in twain; and like saying, 'Stand aside, come not nigh to God' to those who are 'made nigh by the blood of Christ.' "

The book of Hebrews teaches us that we have a better covenant, a better Mediator, a better hope, better promises, a better homeland, a better priesthood, and better possessions — better than the best that Judaism could offer. It assures us that we have eternal redemption, eternal salvation, an eternal covenant, and an eternal inheritance.

It warns solemnly against the sin of apostasy. If a person professes to be a Christian, associates with a Christian assembly, then turns away from Christ and joins those who are enemies of the Lord, it is impossible for such a one to be renewed to repentance.

The Hebrew Epistle encourages true Christians to walk by faith and not by sight because this is the life that pleases Christ. It also encourages us to bear up steadfastly under sufferings, trials, and persecutions in order that we might receive the promised reward.

The Epistle teaches that because of their many privileges, Christians have a very special responsibility.

The superiorities of Christ make them the most highly favored people in the world. If such privileges are neglected, they will suffer loss accordingly at the judgment seat of Christ. More is expected of them than of those who lived under the law; and more will be required in a coming day.

"Therefore let us go forth to Him outside the camp, bearing abuse for Him" (13:13).

BIBLIOGRAPHY

Bruce, A.B. *The Epistle to the Hebrews.* London: T. & T. Clark, 1899.

Gaebelein, A.C. *The Annotated Bible.* Neptune, New Jersey: Loizeaux Brothers, rev. ed. 1970.

Govett, Robert. *Christ Superior to Angels, Moses and Aaron.* London: J. Nisbet, 1884.

Grant, F.W. *The Numerical Bible.* Neptune, New Jersey: Loizeaux Brothers, 1891-1903.

Henderson, G.D. *Studies in the Epistle to the Hebrews.* Barkingside, England: G.F. Vallance, n.d.

Ironside, H.A. *Hebrews and Titus.* Neptune, New Jersey: Loizeaux Brothers, 1932.

Jowett, J.H. *Life in the Heights.* London: Hodder & Stroughton, 1925.

Jukes, Andrew. *The Law of the Offerings.* London: Lamp Press, 1954.

Kelly, William. *Introductory Lectures to the Epistle to the Hebrews and the Epistle to Philemon.* Oak Park, Illinois: Bible Truth Publishers, n.d.

Landis, G.M. *Epistle to the Hebrews: On to Maturity.* Oak Park: Emmaus Bible School, 1964.

Lang, G.H. *The Epistle to the Hebrews.* London: Paternoster Press.

Lenski, R.C.H. *The Interpretation of the Epistle to the Hebrews and of the Epistle of James.* Minneapolis: Augsburg Publishing House, 1938.

Lincoln, William. *Lectures on the Epistle to the Hebrews.* Boston: Believers' Book-Room, n.d.

Mackintosh, C.H. *Notes on Genesis.* Neptune, New Jersey: Loizeaux Brothers, 1880.

Mantle, J.G. *Better Things.* New York: Christian Alliance Publishing Co., 1921.

Meyer, F.B. *The Way into the Holiest.* Grand Rapids: Zondervan Publishing House, 1950.

Murray, Andrew. *The Holiest of All.* Westwood, New Jersey: Revell, 1960.

Newell, W.R. *Hebrews Verse by Verse.* Chicago: Moody Press, 1947.

Ridout, Samuel. *Lectures on the Epistle to the Hebrews.* Neptune, New Jersey: Loizeaux Brothers, 1903.

Saphir, Adolph. *The Epistle to the Hebrews.* Neptune, New Jersey: Loizeaux Brothers, 1946.

Vine, W.E. *The Epistle to the Hebrews.* London: Oliphants Ltd., 1952.

Weatherhead, Leslie D. *Prescription for Anxiety.* London: Hodder & Stoughton, 1956.

Williams, George. *The Student's Commentary on the Holy Scriptures.* Grand Rapids: Kregel Publications, 1953.

Wuest, K.S. *Hebrews in the Greek New Testament.* Grand Rapids: Eerdmans Publishing Co., 1947.